This fascinating journey of one man's discovery of the transformational benefits of TM should be on every leader's reading list.

RAMANI AYER
RETIRED CEO, THE HARTFORD FINANCIAL SERVICES GROUP SINCE 1973

In this inspiring book, Mack Travis takes us along on his personal journey of discovery and mastery of Transcendental Meditation. I highly recommend this compelling work to both beginners and experienced practitioners.

ROBIN L. DAVISSON, PHD
THE ANDREW DICKSON WHITE PROFESSOR OF MOLECULAR PHYSIOLOGY
CORNELL UNIVERSITY

The Expansion of Happiness is a heartfelt and useful primer—perfect for anyone interested in exploring the simple mystery of Transcendental Meditation. Mack Travis uses his thorough knowledge of the history and practice of TM to explain how the meditation practice can transform any life.

AMY DICKINSON
NATIONALLY SYNDICATED COLUMNIST (ASK AMY); PANELIST ON NPR'S
COMEDY QUIZ SHOW "WAIT WAIT DON'T TELL ME", AND AUTHOR OF
THE MIGHTY QUEENS OF FREEVILLE

As a Vietnam veteran, meditating was invaluable in helping me manage what is now recognized as post-traumatic stress (disorder). Mack's book explains how it all works.

STEVE KELLER
FOUNDER WOODHOUSE, THE TIMBER FRAME COMPANY AND
THE MURUS COMPANY

The Expansion of Happiness is a self-help guide at its finest. From a man who walks the walk, Mack Travis presents a compelling and honest look that will open your eyes to the positive effects of Transcendental Meditation.

CARL MAZZOCONE
PRESIDENT, MAINLINE PICTURES, LOS ANGELES, CALIFORNIA

continued

Our minds are difficult to describe and explain…Travis brilliantly gets around this problem by using metaphors to describe…the mind in meditation. This wonderful book is a rhapsody of metaphors that will help the reader to understand how meditation can settle and calm the mind and expand personal happiness.

RON LEIFER, MD, MA
PSYCHIATRIST, PRACTICING BUDDHIST, AUTHOR OF *THE HAPPINESS PROJECT*,
VINEGAR INTO HONEY, ENGAGEMENTS WITH THE WORLD

For anyone seeking the road to success in life, *The Expansion of Happiness* provides the map. Based on an intensely personal journey, Travis describes a simple, accessible meditation technique that leads to better health, more effective action, and personal fulfillment. An essential read.

CHARLES TRAUTMANN, PHD
EXECUTIVE DIRECTOR, SCIENCENTER, ITHACA, NEW YORK

East meets West as Mack Travis writes: "Meditation is accepted in the Indian culture much the same way that prayer is accepted in our Western, predominantly Judeo-Christian, culture." (One can use) Mack's book as a stepping stone for discovery…

WENDY T. WALLACE, PRESIDENT
CHRISTIAN MESSAGE THROUGH ART,
GREENSBORO, NC

As a Doctor of Chiropractic, I discuss the benefits of meditation with nearly every patient. For those who choose to embark on this journey towards the expansion of happiness, I cannot think of a better vehicle than the combination of learning TM and this book to propel one headlong onto that path.

AMMITAI WOROB DC
ITHACA, NEW YORK

There are many excellent books about TM, but Mack's is unique in its down-to-earth and personal style. It is full of good stories that bring his points home in a simple, powerful way. Most of all, you are left with the feeling that it's not just talk, but the heartfelt reflections of a wise man of enormous integrity. There is an unmistakable coherence between the man and his message.

JOEL WYSONG, PHD.
NORTHEAST REGIONAL DIRECTOR, MAHARISHI FOUNDATION USA

THE
EXPANSION OF
HAPPINESS

THE
EXPANSION OF
HAPPINESS

....

A Common-Sense Look at
the Transcendental Meditation Technique
Founded by Maharishi Mahesh Yogi

Mack Travis

TADORNA PRESS
ITHACA • NEW YORK

First published in the United States of America in 2014 by Tadorna Press, Ithaca NY
Text © 2014 by Mack Travis
Cover image © 2014 PhotoDisc, Inc.

Project Manager: Della R. Mancuso, Mancuso Associates Inc.
Creative Director: Mary Kornblum / CMYK Design Inc.
Editing: Rick Ball
Production: Jeffrey Stern

ISBN: 978-0-9915781-0-8 Paperback
978-0-9915781-2-2 E-book

Printed and bound in the United States by Worzalla, Stevens Point, Wisconsin

Appendix A: from Scientific Research on the TM and TM-Sidhi programs, © 2011 by Maharishi University of Management Press, Fairfield Iowa. Reprinted with Permission.

Appendix B: "Evidence Suggests That Meditation Should Be Included In Government-Sponsored Health Programs" is used with permission of Medical News Today.

Second Printing 2015

2 3 4 5 6 7 8 9 10

THIS BOOK IS DEDICATED TO YOU.

ACKNOWLEDGMENTS

My thanks and appreciation go to the friends and family members who have contributed their expertise and opinions to the shaping of this book: Holly Menino Bailey, Rolf Erickson, Kate Travis, Cathy Brotz, and Paul Velleman; sailing buddies and friends Rick and Jane Meisenbach for their encouragement; Sam Katz; my sister and her husband Wendy and Larry Wallace for their comments; to Della Mancuso, for her assistance in publishing and bringing a truly professional team to the project—editor Rick Ball and designer Mary Kornblum; and to my wife and companion of thirty years, Carol Griggs Travis; our DSB, and so many others to whom I remain profoundly grateful.

Above all, my appreciation, respect, and gratitude go to Maharishi Mahesh Yogi, for his selfless devotion to mankind. His technique of Transcendental Meditation® has transformed the lives of millions of people by changing the conviction that we are meant to suffer to a realization that the purpose of life is the expansion of happiness.

His simple formula of meditating twice a day with the Transcendental Meditation technique and "taking it as it comes" has relieved countless individuals of overwhelming stress and freed them to experience life in happiness and become all they can be.

CONTENTS

PREFACE

....

What Is It that Makes You Happy?

Think about it. When in your life have you felt the greatest happiness?

Accomplishment, recognition, confidence, helping others, love—all these have probably contributed to your moments of happiness.

What is it that keeps us from being happy? Wrong action, confusion, not getting what we want, fear, anger, stress? If you have been looking for a way to reduce stress in your life, increase happiness in your life, and find a deeper understanding of yourself, then Transcendental Meditation may be for you. If you are already successful and happy, Transcendental Meditation can bring you even more success and happiness.

Transcendental Meditation (TM) is an effective, effortless meditation technique which quickly enables those who learn it to achieve a quiet heart and a sense of well-being. It is not a religion. It is not a belief system. It is a simple mental technique easily learned in four two-hour sessions with a trained teacher. It is practiced twice a day for fifteen to twenty minutes, morning and evening.

Although one cannot learn the TM technique from a book, this common-sense introduction to TM will provide the background, describing how this remarkably simple technique was brought to the West, from the mountains of the Himalayas in 1958, by Maharishi Mahesh Yogi. It will become apparent how

TM fits into and compares with our traditional Western spiritual paths. The scientific research on TM verifies the improvements in mental and physical health and the improvements in well-being experienced by the millions of people who practice it. This book will give you a clearer sense of how it can effectively improve *your* life.

The practice of TM involves no change in lifestyle. It does not require that one "believe in it" for it to be effective. It is compatible with every religion and every path of life. In fact, many people find that the practice of Transcendental Meditation enhances their understanding and experience of their own beliefs. Whether you are an atheist, an agnostic, or confirmed in a religious practice, be it Eastern or Western, you will find Transcendental Meditation a powerful form of meditation which will quickly and effectively release stress in your life and lead you to clearer thinking, spontaneous right action, and a more positive approach to life.

I began TM nearly forty years ago and have practiced it twice a day since the day I learned. It has brought clearer thought, expanded happiness, wonderful success, and well-being into my work and my relationships. Based on my own experience and the experience of hundreds of people I know who have benefited from the practice of TM, I assure you that learning Transcendental Meditation will be the best investment you will ever make for your own self-development.

INTRODUCTION

....

Transcendental Meditation

How do we take what might be dismissed as a subjective experience and convince a Western intellectual that it is verifiable, that it is consistently reproducible, and that it is common to millions of people? It's probably not that different from "believing" in love. If we have experienced being in love, we know that it is a miraculously supportive, blissfully delightful cure-all for the shortcomings and inadequacies of our life. Being in love cannot be measured scientifically, but if we have experienced it, we know the sense of completeness and confidence, the elation and euphoria, the contentment and peace that descend upon us once we have found the someone who will reflect back our most perfect self in love.

Being in love is a unique experience, but it is also a subjective experience. It takes place in our own mind and heart. Others can observe its results in the erectness of our walk, the smile and bliss on our face, the assertiveness and sense of fun it produces in us. Shyness disappears and is replaced by a coy attractiveness and openness. But is being in love measurable?

Who cares if it's measurable? We just enjoy experiencing it. It may be subjective, but it makes us more fun to be around. It gives us immense pleasure, but it is private and it is ours. We don't need to have our experience verified. We don't care to measure it. We know it is real, and that is enough for us.

So it is with Transcendental Meditation. It has been measured and researched. It has been scientifically verified as the experience of a distinct state of consciousness, but in a sense, who cares? TM is simply the most effective tool for stress release that many of us have ever found or will ever find. We are not required to have faith in it for it to change our life. We simply do the technique and the benefits of well-being, successful action, and happiness will follow—much like being in love.

Imagine a small dark-skinned Indian man, hardly over five feet tall, with long hair and long beard, dressed in sandals and a flowing white robe, stepping off the plane in San Francisco. He knows no one. He has only the name of one contact, but he has arrived on the first stage of a trip to go around the world to tell people about life in bliss, that there is no need to suffer. His message: It is mankind's right and natural state to be happy. There is a fourth state of consciousness, Transcendental Consciousness. And he promises that anyone can access it through meditating with the technique he teaches. He has made no plans in advance— where to stay, what to eat, where to go after San Francisco—and he has no money. The year is 1959.

The contact in San Francisco introduces Maharishi to his friends, and word spreads quickly about this guru who has arrived from India. He holds lecture after lecture telling people of his Spiritual Regeneration Movement, and he teaches his Transcendental Meditation technique. It is a small fire at first, but the warmth spreads. Students pick it up. The *Los Angeles Times* does a full-page spread on this "Indian Guru" who has come to the United States to tell his good news about life in bliss—but it is a subjective experience.

As a young man, Maharishi felt drawn to find a spiritual teacher. He found one of the highest spiritual figures in India: *Guru Dev* (respected teacher). Encouraged by his teacher, Maharishi completed his university degree in physics, after which he spent twelve years, as he says, "at the lotus feet of Guru Dev."

Shortly after Maharishi first met his teacher, Guru Dev

became the *Shankaracharya* of Northern India, the head of one of the four principal seats of the Vedic tradition of India, which offers integrated knowledge of life in all its truth and fullness. Guru Dev's full title became His Divinity Swami Brahmananda Saraswati, Jagad Guru, Bhagwan Shankaracharya of Jyotir Math.

After Guru Dev's passing in 1953, Maharishi retired to the Valley of the Saints, high in the Himalayas. He tells the story of how, after several years of silent meditation, he began feeling an impulse to journey to a temple in Rameshvaram in the south of India. An older recluse with whom he shared this thought discouraged him from going out into the world, so Maharishi let the thought go. But from time to time it returned, and he expressed it again. Finally, after hearing it a number of times, the elder recluse told him to just go, act on the thought, then return and never think of it again.

Dressed in his white robe, the traditional garb of a *Brahmachari* (celibate), Maharishi made the long journey to the south of India. Having left the peace and solitude of his life in the Valley of the Saints, and having completed his pilgrimage to the main temples of the South, he had the realization that "there is such a gap between what life is declared to be and what life is found to be." He was moved by the thought that it is not necessary for man to suffer.

"I was so naturally and deeply moved between the two realities: life being lived on a completely wretched level and life described on the most exalted level. And there was no reason why there should be a gap, because it's so simple for the individual to be on that level of universality and immortality. It's so simple. This was the natural feeling that was deep in my mind, that something should be done so that people don't suffer, because there is no reason to suffer."

Maharishi had the thought that it might be good to give the blessing of the Himalayas to the people of the South before returning north. In the city of Trivandrum, a man stopped him on the street and asked, "Do you speak?" Maharishi answered, "I do, but do you mean lecturing? I don't," and continued on.

Nevertheless, the man found Maharishi again later that day and announced that he had arranged a series of seven lectures for him at the local library, a prestigious place that often hosted distinguished speakers. In response to the man's questioning about what he would speak about, Maharishi outlined seven topics and the man wrote them down. When the man got up to go, Maharishi said, "Leave a copy with me!"

So each evening, Maharishi went to the library and spoke, and each evening the size of the audience doubled, eager to hear that man's natural state is one of happiness and bliss. They came, they listened, and Maharishi taught them the simple technique of Transcendental Meditation. More and more people came to hear him speak and to learn this simple and effective form of meditation. After this, he was asked to speak again and again throughout India.

Meditation is accepted in the Indian culture much the same way that prayer is accepted in our Western, predominantly Judeo-Christian, culture. People don't question its effectiveness or subjectivity; they simply do it. Here was a man offering an effortless and effective method of meditation which produced positive results quickly and spontaneously in one's daily life. Meditate with this technique of Transcendental Meditation, Maharishi said, and stress will be released; you will think more clearly, your daily activity will be more successful, and you will become happier and more fulfilled. It is a path to spiritual development. And people found that what he said was true. Their lives did become happier and more fulfilling as they practiced TM.

Maharishi tells that he once again had the thought that he must reach a larger audience, must reach the entire world with his message that life is bliss and can be lived without suffering. His followers raised the money for his plane fare, and he began the first of what would become five around-the-world tours over the next decade, giving out his message and teaching the Transcendental Meditation technique.

In his early lectures in the United States, Maharishi mentioned the physical benefits associated with TM—better rest, deeper sleep, and reduced stress. The first newspaper articles reported that this bearded Indian guru had come to tell us how to get better sleep. At first, Maharishi found his reception in the United States discouraging. Here he was, providing a technique to produce life in enlightenment—life without suffering, life in bliss. He was teaching that the purpose of life is the expansion of happiness, and what was important to the American audience was a good night's sleep!

Maharishi began to realize that it would be beneficial to perform scientific research on the physiological and psychological results of practicing Transcendental Meditation. This would help to convince people in the West that this subjective experience of transcending in meditation and the benefits that it produced in all areas of life, both personal and beyond, was a unique and measurable state of mind and being.

Robert Keith Wallace, a UCLA doctoral student in physiology, took up the challenge. In 1970, he published his first study in the journal *Science*. The study indicated that during the practice of the Transcendental Meditation technique a unique physiological state is attained that produces profound rest as measured by decreased oxygen consumption, decreased heart rate, and increased basal skin resistance, an indicator of resistance to stress. Today, Dr. Wallace, who also did postdoctoral research at Harvard Medical School, is the author of two books—*The Neurophysiology of Enlightenment* and *The Physiology of Consciousness*—has lectured in over fifty countries around the world, and is recognized as a pioneering researcher in the neurophysiology of higher states of consciousness.

In the ensuing years, researchers have performed more than six hundred physiological and psychological studies on the benefits of Transcendental Meditation for the individual's physical and mental well-being, as well as its effects on society. These studies have been gathered and reprinted in a seven-volume series titled *Scientific Research on Maharishi's Transcendental Meditation and TM-Sidhi Program: Collected Papers.*

Maharishi not only saw the need for scientific research to verify for the Westerner how unique and effective his technique is, but he also felt the need to, as he put it, "multiply himself." If he was going to reach the entire world with his knowledge that life is not meant to be lived in suffering, that the purpose of life is expansion of happiness, that stress is the impediment to living life to its fullest, and that his technique of meditation is the effective solution to stress reduction, then he needed to train thousands of teachers to teach his Transcendental Meditation.

He began an international series of courses to train teachers in his methods. He held courses in Majorca, Spain; Seelisberg, Switzerland; Estes Park, Colorado; and dozens of other locations. Students came by the thousands. In 1972, he developed his World Plan for teaching TM to the entire world. His lectures were recorded and videotaped, and eventually thousands of his students became certified teachers of the Transcendental Meditation program. He had truly "multiplied himself"!

What began as Maharishi's recurring thought deep in the Himalayas has now spread around the world, and there are Transcendental Meditation centers in many countries. There are schools where the students learn TM as part of their curriculum in India; China; Cambodia; Fairfield, Iowa; and scores of other locations. Forty thousand teachers have been trained to teach TM and over six million people have learned the technique since Maharishi first set out on his journey and began to undertake the spiritual regeneration of the world.

During the early years of bringing out to the world the knowledge he had gained from Guru Dev, he came to be known as "His Holiness Maharishi Mahesh Yogi." A *Rishi* is a "seer" of the Veda ("knowledge" in Sanskrit), one who is able to cognize knowledge directly. A *Maharishi*, or "Great Seer," is one who applies that knowledge for the good of mankind. The term *Yogi* means "one who is united with the Self."

For those who practice Transcendental Meditation, it is reassuring to hear that this personal experience of transcending has been scientifically verified as a fourth state of consciousness, different from the three we are so familiar with—waking, dreaming, and sleeping. But like being in love, it doesn't matter greatly, for the experience is so pleasurable we just enjoy both the transcendence in meditation and the increased effectiveness and expansion of happiness in our lives.

For those who have not learned Transcendental Meditation, there is ample scientific research to prove its validity and effectiveness in one's life. The *Absolute* that one reaches in transcending—this universal field of consciousness—becomes integrated into the relative, the workaday world that comprises our daily existence. Both the personal experience of millions and the hundreds of scientific research studies show that in this practice of Transcendental Meditation we have an effective tool to assist us in reaching our full potential in daily life.

In this book you will read why this technique matters to you. You will come to understand how you, too, can release the stress in your life through meditation and experience that your natural "state of Being" is one of happiness and bliss. This book will present the common-sense case for why you, too, should consider learning TM—the Transcendental Meditation technique.

ONE

OUR HUMAN CONDITION

....

Life means action—no one can escape activity.
This being so, it is wise to know not only what one is going to do,
but where, as a result, one is going to end up.

MAHARISHI,
BHAGAVAD-GITA: A NEW TRANSLATION
AND COMMENTARY
(Chapter IV, Verse 17)

As a young man in the 1960s, I searched through the many typical ways the young find to create themselves. Who was I? What should I do with my life? Were the answers to be found intellectually, spiritually, sensually, or in a combination of all three? I crashed on the rocks more than once. Don't we all at one time or another?

• • •

For me, as for so many others, Transcendental Meditation became the answer to my search. Today, TM has reached into all strata of society. Meditation is recognized as a balancer, a technique for creating peace, self-realization, and fulfillment in one's life. In my younger years I was an actor, then a college instructor, and after that, a filmmaker. Eventually, I became a successful real estate developer and businessman. Others I have known who learned TM found success as doctors, lawyers, teachers, electricians, artists, parents, ministers, space scientists, professional athletes—in dozens of different walks of life. Our human condition is shaped and remedied by action, and TM clears our head and lets us act unencumbered, freed from the baggage of our youth and our indiscretions. For me, as for so many, it has become the tool whereby we find answers to our search.

Our mind and ability to reason can usually save us from con artists, foolish choices, and imaginary solutions. But in my experience, our mind and reason can also play tricks, leading us into endless, meaningless dead ends and self-delusion. It is not by talk but by actions that we are known and that others are known to us. It is our actions that create who we are in the world, and it is our thoughts, desires, and skills that will determine the effectiveness of our actions.

Think back to the teachers, parents, friends, and relatives who have guided and shaped your thinking. As intelligent, rational, spiritual, and scientific as we are today, we are part of a civilization that has evolved over millennia. Like it or not, we do not simply stand alone, the product of our own growth. Each of us is dependent on those around us who have nourished, trained, and guided us. We may feel we are a "hotshot," but none of us is completely self-made, and none of us is an infallible superman or superwoman. Yet every one of us is unique. Every one of us will make our own contribution in life, and every one of us who follows "the path of personal evolution" will eventually find his or her own way.

It is possible to reason ourselves into a box that absorbs us, not realizing that our reason is limited in its scope to the box itself. One can take flights of fantasy into the spiritual, with or without guides. One can trip into the seemingly boundless with the drug of choice, should one be so inclined, and one can and does suffer the eventual consequences.

We yearn for the total certainty and self-confidence that we may find in our religious experiences or in the first love we experience as we find our sexuality. We exist in an endless sea of emotions, ideas, relationships, successes, and failures, all pushing and pulling us in directions we sometimes find comfortable, sometimes uncomfortable. Yet we are alive. We must act. We must take those halting first steps to find our identity and our happiness.

And we do act. We seek. We find pleasure. And sometimes we go out of balance. Like a rat with electrodes implanted in the pleasure center of our brain, we can tap and tap the bar until we become completely overloaded, completely carried away. The stimulus can be alcohol, sex, anything in excess. It is a good time, but looking back we see that it offered little in the way of lasting or beneficial results, little that contributed to our growth and evolution.

We may find a direct relationship with God, or total unity with a lover, or a sense of invincibility from a new job or the recent successes we have had. The conversion, the breakthrough, the glamour, the certainty that we feel lasts temporarily, and then, for many of us, it fades away. And if it does, we feel innately drawn to find it again, to seek unity with something greater than our selves, something that will enhance our self beyond our current limitations. We yearn for whatever it is that will give us a sense of completeness, wholeness, and happiness.

We may seek it through love and devotion. We may seek it through hard work and discipline. It may come. We may find it. If we do find it, we will grasp it. We will glory in it, but as always, eventually it will fade. As it fades, we can feel let down, depressed, alienated from our Self. We may try to recapture it with the ineffective—more sex, or the temporary peace and unity induced by a drug—and as exciting as it all seems for a while, the end result is that it is ineffective in producing lasting unity, lasting certainty, lasting happiness.

For the religious, this alienation can be the dark night of the soul. For the lover, it can be the loss of the love of our life. For the man of action, it may be the lack of a project, lack of direction, and the depression that ensues from the inability to make a choice and move forward.

It is the hangover. It is the self-induced gloom of failure that follows. We were certain we were in love, certain we were invincible in our project or business. These were the peak experiences of our life. Where did they go, this sense of certainty, this freedom from inhibition, this super confidence, this presence of love, this presence of God?

For many of us they have disappeared. Disappeared into our sense of failure, our lack of confidence, our certainty that we are now depressed, doomed, and at least for the moment, damned. And we are less than sure what to do next.

We may drag our self out of the morass to continue. Or we may not. We may seek help. Or we may simply continue in our depression. We may seek a teacher, a mentor, a counselor. We may seek renewal in our religion or a new love affair. We may simply seek the new—the new job, the new partner, the new home—something outside of ourselves that we hope will make us feel complete. We are after all alive. We must act.

We may find our self pressing the bar again and again in different ways. We may pray or demand. We may turn furious, or we may retreat into personal despair and solace, licking our wounds, uncertain of our place in the world. Eventually we will find that pressing the bar no longer works. The pleasure center is so worn out from overwork that it is rendered useless. We need a break. We need time to recover.

We may give up, or we may accept the religious explanation: We are sinners; we are guilty. Or we may try the intellectual solution: Study harder; read more; think more. Or the emotional solution: Find more lovers. Or the businessman's solution: Do more deals; make more money. Then I'll be happier.

Or we may try a solution from the ancient Vedic tradition of India—finding the answer as did the Beatles after spending time in Rishikesh, India, with Maharishi in 1968, when they sang so simply, "Let it be," and we may learn to "take it as it comes."

Western intellectual and religious traditions have formed our cultural heritage and thinking for over 2,500 years. The Greeks found truth with Plato, and his essence of perfection, and the pantheon of Greek gods; the Romans with theirs. The truth of the Christian tradition was shaped and eventually institutionalized into the Catholic Church. It was, in turn, reacted to and reshaped by the Protestants in the Reformation. Truth was sought and found in the reason of the Enlightenment. And truth was shattered in the Inquisition. Science and philosophy re-emerged as the sources and methods of arriving at truth—all this, as if truth will bring us the happiness we seek.

Philosophers, scientists, religious leaders, mystics, and psychiatrists continue to give us one complex proposal after another in an attempt to explain the world and how it works, the human condition, what it is, and how to manipulate it for our happiness, or give in to it with acceptance and live with our despair.

What matters through it all, what cuts through all the philosophy and science, all the mysticism and complex ideas, is a personal relationship with our Self. It is this, we eventually realize, that determines whether we will be happy or miserable, successful or unsuccessful, as we act to perform our "dharma," our duty in life. We are responsible for ourselves, and we are responsible for finding the relationship with our greater Self.

We can try to shift responsibility off to God—out there somewhere—who will save us, make us happy, make us productive, and we may be able to find him in our prayers, but we may also find that God is elusive. God is unexplainable. Perhaps we find that God, in an often jumbled religious understanding, is either "dead" or inaccessible in any consistent and meaningful way. The rituals may help. The social relationships in the Church may help. But we may also find we are surrounded by a secular society, thrown this way and that by circumstances that leave us searching and uncertain as to the presence of God.

We can shift responsibility for well-being and happiness off to our work, the striving for excellence, for success, for recognition. We can shift it off to our reason, the intellectual certainties that will temporarily help us find ourselves and last until the next better idea comes along. We can shift it off to our lovers and friends—"Make me happy!" We can do that on all fronts. We can look temporarily to our histories, our novels, traditions, and travels, and although they become temporary diversions, they are quickly over and out of our consciousness, gone from our tools for producing well-being. Our daily routine once again takes over, and we find ourselves lost again in the unawareness and stresses of daily life.

Each one of us must begin with this personal relationship with our self. If we fail to find our Self at our center, we will be forever catapulted off the walls of our ideas and surroundings. A long history of thought, religion, and tradition will continue to bind us, limit us, suffocate and confuse us in our search for consistent contentment, consistent happiness.

We must find our own way. We are responsible for creating our own happiness. We must make our own contribution.

The human condition is a constant search for Self, the Self at our center, for who we are, for what actions we should take, for what will make us happy. Talk is indeed cheap, and we want action—effective, decisive action that we can trust and rely on— for it is by our actions that we are known, and in the end it is our actions that will lead us to happiness and fulfillment.

Transcendental Meditation is a simple technique that releases stress in our mind and body, allowing us to think more clearly. Thus our actions become more successful, and we can effectively fulfill our desires, which leads us to our personal happiness.

Meditation → Release of Stress → Clear Thought →
Successful Action → Fulfillment of Desires → Personal Happiness

Our concept of God, even our concept of no God, hovers over our life. We can be in love or not in love, successful at the moment in business or not, but in the meantime, because we practice TM, we are thinking clearly and are able to act more effectively and efficiently than before.

Transcendental Meditation can be the one simple, effective tool which will allow the mind to experience the silence within. More and more silence gets infused, resulting in clearer thinking and action more in accord with our dharma, our duty in life. Through TM, our awareness opens to the happiness and fulfillment found in the realization of the Self at our core. Our actions spontaneously become more effective, more successful.

To quote Maharishi: "Life means action—no one can escape activity. This being so, it is wise to know not only what one is going to do, but where, as a result, one is going to end up."

TWO

DHARMA AND THE DOUBLE BIND

....

*"Dharma" signifies the path of evolution.
The practice of Yoga is a direct way to evolution. Through it,
the individual mind gains the state of Cosmic Intelligence.*

MAHARISHI,
BHAGAVAD-GITA: A NEW TRANSLATION AND COMMENTARY
(Chapter II, Verse 40)

It took me into my thirties to accept the fact that no matter how hard I tried, I was doomed to failure unless I took responsibility for my own actions. Was I a failure? I felt like it. I had left my wife and children for another woman. That lasted a while, and it crashed. The untenable strain of loving one person and wanting to be with another broke me. How in God's name do you make a choice? What is the right choice? Which person? Which job? It seemed impossible to know. In my imagined strength and inflated ego, I had thrown out religious guidance; I had thrown out societal morals, and I was on my own flying blind in a furious storm. After learning TM, and after reading in Maharishi's commentary on the *Bhagavad-Gita* that we each have a duty in life, a dharma that it is our responsibility to find, it was like being asked in Sunday School, What do you want to be? What is God calling you to do? Perhaps there might be a meaningful direction out there. Perhaps? Somewhere? It was my responsibility to find it.

• • •

In his translation and commentary on the *Bhagavad-Gita*, Maharishi Mahesh Yogi illuminates the ancient story of Arjuna, a great warrior who is driven onto the battlefield in his chariot by Lord Krishna to confront the opposing army. As it turns out, the opposing army is made up of Arjuna's relatives, who are attempting to overthrow the kingdom which it is Arjuna's duty as the greatest archer of his time to defend. It is his duty—his *dharma*—to fight. He knows this in his mind, yet in his heart he feels intense love for his kinsmen. How can he confront and kill his loved ones? Arjuna broods on this conflict between his heart and his mind, and he is unable to choose which path to follow. Finally, in despair, he throws down his weapons, incapacitated by the dilemma confronting him.

The dynamic of Arjuna's situation is the classic "double bind" with which we are all familiar. There are times in our lives when we find ourselves confronted with moral dilemmas, choices to which there is no satisfactory answer. The dictates of our emotions and our heart conflict with the rational directives of our mind, and we are torn. We know that no matter which choice we make, we will simply be "damned if we do, damned if we don't."

What follows in the verses of the *Bhagavad-Gita* is the story of the resolution of Arjuna's dilemma. His conscience tells him to fulfill his duty; his heart tells him to respect his love of kinsmen. He is unable to make the choice, and in despair he cries out to his teacher, Lord Krishna, whom he had chosen to drive his chariot. Krishna is the embodiment of the Absolute. Their 5,000-year-old dialogue becomes one of the world's great books depicting the human condition.

Not dissimilar to the school or university classroom, the teacher needs the student—and the student needs the teacher—for knowledge to flow forth. In his commentary, Maharishi explains the unfamiliar and ancient verses of the *Gita* in language that is accessible, and he identifies and draws out the underlying dynamics that lead to the path of meditation and transcendence as the solution to our own dilemmas, our own double binds.

As Maharishi states in his commentary on the *Gita*, "Dharma signifies the path of evolution. The practice of Yoga is a direct way to evolution. Through it, the individual mind gains the state of Cosmic Intelligence—that unbounded state of universal Being which is the summit of evolution."

All human beings seeking growth and fulfillment in their lives must follow the path of evolution. The alternative is to dwell in the status quo, if not in actual regression. Each of us has a duty to perform in life—our "dharma" in this world. "Rise up and do your duty"—Lord Krishna's message to Arjuna—turns out to be the solution to the dilemmas of our own double binds. As with

Arjuna, however, the dictates of heart and the dictates of mind can often lead us in differing directions and can indeed lead to irresolvable mental and emotional conflict. But when it comes down to the decision of which to follow, the heart or the mind, it is simply our duty to perform *our duty in life*—that which will promote maximum evolution and growth to ourselves and our society—our dharma.

But how do we determine dharma? How do we know what we must do in life? How do we know for certain what our duty is? Maharishi refers to Yoga as union, contact of individual mind with its universal or cosmic source. Hence it follows that the practice of Yoga, or meditation, is the direct way for each of us to realize our personal dharma. As Maharishi further states in his commentary on the *Gita*, "Dharma is natural to man, and so is this practice of Yoga, for it is in accordance with the very nature of the mind and brings fulfillment to life. That is why this Yoga is the dharma of everyone."

Each of us, moment by moment, determines what it is we must do. We may refuse to do it, or we may be unable for some reason to determine what it is we should do in a given situation. In this instance, *no choice* becomes *the choice*, and we will realize the consequences of whatever no choice brings our way.

Life in the relative continually presents us with choices—the duality of right and wrong, black and white, mind and heart, reason and emotion, this way or that way. Maharishi presents us with the teachings of the *Bhagavad-Gita* and discovers within them a technique—a technique for meditating and transcending to a blissful state of mind that he calls *pure consciousness*, the *Absolute*. By allowing the mind to transcend the field of activity and become established in silence, the mind gets infused with pure consciousness, and right action becomes automatic. It is this simple technique of Transcendental Meditation that Maharishi is offering to mankind.

The solution or resolution to double binds, to the need for

certainty, to the desire for unity of heart and action, is the understanding born of transcending and experiencing the bliss found
in the Absolute. It is in this state of "bliss" that all opposites can
coexist, that all dilemmas find their resolution. Simple to say, but
without a reliable technique for experiencing bliss, it is elusive or
impossible to trust that we are there, that what we have found
in our religious experience, or what we have found at the end of
our trail to reason and truth, is really "It"—and the "It" changes.

We can reason ourselves into a box. We can experience God's
presence only to find that it fades. Bliss and certainty come and
go. We are captured by the next idea, the next philosopher who
can destroy the carefully built logic upon which we have come to
rely; the next charismatic leader who can provide the new sense
of ecstasy to sweep us to certainty, at least for a while; or the next
drug that can satisfy our craving for unity and a sense of worth,
temporary as it may be.

There is no permanent solution. We are after all human. We
are easily swayed. We are vulnerable. Our mind and its reasoning
ability protect us to an extent. Our heart, with its ability to sense
the truth, protects us to an extent. But when they are in conflict,
as they were when Arjuna was confronted with the choice that
is no choice, the choice that will bring him to misery whichever
way he chooses—what then? What can be done to put us back
on track when we are lethargic and lost in despair, when we are
paralyzed by the uncertainty and loss of confidence we experience
when we are torn by choices, none of which we want to follow—
the double binds?

Transcendental Meditation is an effortless technique that
involves sitting comfortably for twenty minutes twice a day with
eyes closed and following the simple instructions for meditation
given by a trained teacher of TM. There is no one right experience of TM. Experiences will vary from session to session. During
the course of instruction, the teacher will go over all the possible experiences in meditation. As we settle down and stress is

released, we may feel a peaceful relaxation descending over us. We may experience that we are "there"—there at the silence, the Self at our center. It is effortless. It is simple. Yet it is profoundly powerful.

Perform the technique and it relaxes us; it clears our mind. We come out of meditation energized, clear-headed, and ready for action, for we have experienced a deep rest and a deep sense of clarity. We have transcended the world of boundaries, the world of opposites, the world of double binds. Our decisions come more easily now, for our dharma is more apparent. We have experienced a state of being in which opposites seem to be resolved and the path forward is open. We stand poised and ready for our next move.

It is remarkable that there is no effort required to practice Transcendental Meditation. Contrary to traditional thought about meditation, it is not necessary to meditate for years to enjoy the experience of transcending, of going beyond the surface level of thought to deeper and deeper levels of the thinking process. This technique works from the start; it works with the very first meditation. Instruction by a certified teacher, trained in the TM technique, assures us in a few sessions that we are taking the proper "dive within," that we are meditating correctly, and then the technique is our own. For the rest of our life, it is ours to do.

Transcendental Meditation, done properly, is so enjoyable that you will look forward to your twenty-minute, twice-a-day meditations. It is so simple, so natural. Once you have transcended, the enjoyment is so profound when you have experienced this state of consciousness that you have no desire to get involved in some other byway.

It is remarkable that there is no faith or belief involved for Transcendental Meditation to work. One does not have to "believe in Maharishi." One does not have to believe in God. One does not have to have faith in anything to achieve the rest and relief from anxiety, as mental and physical stress dissolves through the practice of this simple meditation technique.

Transcendental Meditation is a mental technique only, and it has been learned and found to be effective by priests, rabbis, monks (both Christian and Buddhist), atheists, and by millions of people from all parts of society and all parts of the world. The practice of TM simply enhances each of us as an individual, and whatever belief system we follow becomes all the more meaningful and delightful.

It is remarkable that the results reported both anecdotally and by scientific research on people practicing Transcendental Meditation are consistent, positive, and continue to grow throughout one's lifetime. People report better sleep, better results in their work, better relationships, better grades, better overall quality of life—in a word, all the things that lead to *greater happiness*.

The scientific research on Transcendental Meditation includes more than six hundred studies in forty countries. Among other benefits, the research shows reduced blood pressure, reduced anxiety, improved performance on tests, reduced alcohol consumption, reduced smoking, better overall health—all proven results that lead to an improved quality of life for those who practice Transcendental Meditation.

The intense drama of Arjuna's double bind, choosing between his duty of defending his kingdom and sparing his kinsmen may not apply directly to us, but we all have moral and practical decisions that must be made on a continual basis.

If we are to be true to ourselves, if we are to follow our own dharma, if we are to get the most we can out of life, it is our responsibility to choose, and to the best of our ability make the most evolutionary choices for our life. As Maharishi states, "The practice of Yoga is a direct way to evolution. Through it, the individual mind gains the state of Cosmic Intelligence."

Transcendental Meditation is a form of Yoga that can quickly and easily take us to the source of thought, to pure consciousness, the Absolute, the "state of Cosmic Intelligence"—and from there we find we have the insight and confidence we need to make the most evolutionary choices in our life. TM is the essence of simplicity. Practice it daily and life's problems begin to work themselves out. The heart values of life—love and compassion, intuition and tolerance—expand. More and more spontaneously, you will be able to do what you know to be right, and not do what you know to be wrong. Through the practice of Transcendental Meditation you will quickly find yourself well on the road to a happy, blissful, and fulfilling life.

THREE

KARMA, AND WHERE ARE WE NOW?

....

*The wise are tools in the hands of the Divine; they innocently
carry out the Divine plan. Their actions arise
from their desire for "the welfare of the world."*

MAHARISHI,
BHAGAVAD-GITA: A NEW TRANSLATION AND COMMENTARY
(Chapter III, Verse 25)

One of my true loves is live theater. Throughout undergraduate and graduate school I studied acting and directing. I worked as an actor for five seasons of summer stock theater and earned my Actors Equity card. In 1968, I joined the ranks of unemployed "professional" actors in New York City and began the rounds of auditions. My life unfolded from there as a temp worker, taxi driver, filmmaker, college instructor, and eventually property owner and real estate developer, but I have always kept a great affection for live theater.

In the summer of 2012, my wife and I attended three performances of *The Rocky Horror Show* within a two-week run at our local Equity summer stock theater. I was both fascinated and horrified at the moral morass it represented—it was theater, and it was all in fun, but in my mind it was a morass nonetheless. I came away wondering if we are to be so shaken up and softened up as a society to accept those ways of life that injure, offend, and cause harm to others? "Do unto others..." "As ye sow, so shall ye reap..." Are these meaningless concepts?

• • •

In 1981, Scottish philosopher Alasdair MacIntyre published a book titled *After Virtue*. He describes our current dilemma in Western society and concludes that, morally, we are operating without a compass. We live in a world of moral relativism where each individual is free to make up his own rules of engagement, and this is a situation fraught with danger.

To reestablish our moral compass, MacIntyre urges a return to "Tradition," a return to the morality of the Catholic Church and the Aristotelian ethics of virtue. In other words, we should look around us at the lack of ethics and the prevalence of greed, self-interest, and selfishness. As a society, we are indeed in many ways lost. MacIntyre strongly suggests that a return to Christian ethics and morality will save us from the pitfalls of moral relativism, where each makes his own morals and values.

Looking at the history of Western thought, Plato described the certainty of form and essence, and Aristotle's reasoning and logic became the basis of Christian thought and explanation. But once Descartes, in his *Discourse on Method* in 1637, cast us free from the authority, dogma, and tradition of the Church with his *cogito, ergo sum*—"I think, therefore I am"—and after much growth and pain, one could say we were intellectually and spiritually free to think for ourselves.

Bacon, Locke, Hume, Kant, and other philosophers took us into the Enlightenment, the Age of Reason. Our intellects soared. With the shackles of authority—the Inquisition of the Church— removed, the sciences evolved, and Western civilization roared forth to new achievements in the modern age that have created so much of the technology and the material world we live in and enjoy today. Western civilization has tried new social structures— Marxism, capitalism and democracy—giant and sometimes halting steps forward from the feudalism and total monarchy of previous centuries. Today, in the West, the individual reigns supreme in our thought.

Today, the "Existential Individual" may imagine that he or she is free to create himself or herself, free of moral restrictions, free of intellectual restrictions, free from religious restrictions. We can make up our own religions; we can even follow the charismatic leader who leads us all the way to Jonestown. It is dangerous territory, this moral relativism. One could say, there is a gap between the "Is" and the "Ought." What *is*, is not necessarily what *ought* to be, but by whose definition?

The Rocky Horror Show is a play written by Richard O'Brien and was first performed in London in 1973. Later it was turned into the cult film *The Rocky Horror Picture Show*. On the surface, the play is a rollicking spoof on horror movies, TV, and pop culture, but in essence it reflects the times: the post-Vietnam era, the epitome of morality thrown into a cocked hat. Family values, marriage, and religion are ridiculed and replaced with a sort of Dionysian romp in which the world of sensual pleasure becomes the accepted norm.

But after the show, after our own hangover, after our own journey into hedonism, after the many paths tried and discarded, after the crushing weight of the divorce and the ensuing depression, after we have overindulged ourselves and felt the ensuing regret—with a little reflection, we must acknowledge that without a moral compass, without a tradition to follow, we are indeed, as O'Brien put it in *The Rocky Horror Show*, "lost in space."

As MacIntyre urges, a return to tradition of some sort might restore our moral compass, but who wants to give up their independence now? Who wants to stop thinking for themselves? Many of us will choose the independence and the risk of danger. We will do our best to think and act for ourselves; tradition and someone else's sense of morality have no claim on us. It is, after all, thrilling to live on the edge. We feel progressive, important, and self-satisfied that we are in the forefront of our peers. We may be steering ahead blindly, but at least it is we who are steering.

Never mind that we are susceptible to the latest fad, easily seduced by greed. We run the risk thereby of living in a state of moral relativism, making our decisions and choices based more and more on what the outcome will do for ourselves and ourselves alone. Others can fend for themselves. We may consider ourselves independent, but the danger and the risk are real.

For those not grounded in the ethics and values of a religious tradition, this can be the world where the Ponzi-scheme con man Bernie Madoff reigns, as he did for twenty years. It is the world where financial scams pile up and cheat and clog the true value of the financial system until it reaches a state of collapse, as finally happened with Madoff in 2008, when he was exposed and received a 150-year prison sentence. My own cousin's broker-age business in New York was a victim of Bernie Madoff; when Madoff was indicted, my cousin and his investors lost billions of dollars. You have only to read *The Wall Street Journal* to know that this is how business can be conducted in the world of moral relativism.

This can be the world of Florida housing shells, where the contractors build the exterior similar to a stage set. My son-in-law, who worked for a Florida contractor, observed this first-hand. The mortgage brokers do a drive-by and value the house as completed, then sell it bundled together in a mortgage-backed security to overseas investors who will never see it. The brokers collect their fees, but there is nothing of value at the core. No one ever went inside to find out what was really there, and the vacant unfinished shell languishes without a resident.

This can be the world of John Perkins and *Confessions of an Economic Hit Man*. Written in 2004, Perkins's book describes his career as a business consultant. Fresh out of college with a degree in economics, he is literally seduced by a female representative of the "corporatocracy" into serving as a well-paid advisor to Third World countries. He is trained to produce overly optimistic financial projections that convince the country's leader—usually the dictator—that he can borrow tremendous amounts of money from the World Bank to improve his country. With the money from the loans, the dictator is shown how to hire the largest con-struction contractors and oil companies in the world—Bechtel, Halliburton, BP, Exxon, and the like—to bring electricity, roads, and supposedly a better life to his country, while the dictator pockets large fees for himself.

Perkins was well trained, and his financial projections of 17 percent annual growth may have looked achievable to the eco-nomically uninitiated (Perkins acknowledges that 3–4 percent growth might have been more reasonable). Coupled with an intense sales job and huge fees to the dictator and a prospectus that appeared reasonable in a dream state of expansion, the country was off to the races. In *Confessions*, he acknowledges that his projections were, by design, always impossibly optimistic. When, according to plan, the dictator's government is no longer able to service the unreasonable debt, the country defaults on its loans. The corporations have made fortunes from developing the country's infrastructure with the borrowed money, but the targeted country is now in default. Since they can no longer pay their loans, the country is now at the mercy of the large corporations and the World Bank (read United States Government).

The country now has roads, dams, and electrical power, all of the infrastructure necessary for development of its natural resources (read oil, forests, and minerals). And of course, since the country is in default on its loans, it must—as a good defaulted debtor—do whatever the holders of the debt dictate. If the leader does not cooperate, as Omar Torrijos in Panama refused to do in 1981, Perkins explains that "the jackals" (read CIA) are sent in, and the leader is simply blown up during a ride in his private airplane. Or a coup or a rigged election is instigated, and a new, more favorable leader is installed, one who will cooperate with the oil companies and the mega-corporations in the rape of his country.

After thirty-five years and tremendous financial success in his career, Perkins's sense of guilt overcomes him, and he tells all in *Confessions of an Economic Hit Man*. This is one example of how business can be conducted in the world of moral relativism.

As a draft-worthy college student in 1967, I lived through the Vietnam era. My friends and I marched down Broadway in New York City to protest what we saw as the senselessness of this CIA-instigated war. And today we know this to be the world of *Legacy of Ashes: The History of the CIA* written by the *New York Times* reporter and Pulitzer Prize winner Tim Weiner. Based on his reading of more than fifty thousand now-declassified documents from the archives of the CIA, the White House, and the

State Department, Weiner sets out to depict the sorry state of the U.S. intelligence service. In so doing, he shocks us with the gruesome tragedies of secrecy, deceit, and behind-the-scenes decision making that produced the Bay of Pigs, Vietnam, and Iran-Contra, as well as the sham governments and major coups of the world, orchestrated by the CIA, that have left us with 9/11 and the wars in Iraq and Afghanistan. But this is how business is conducted in the world of moral relativism.

Our country was founded as "The Republic of Virtue"— Life, Liberty, Justice for all. Our founding values ensure each of us freedom, opportunity, the right to speak our mind without oppression. We are the haven for the world's oppressed. We are the country where the lowly and obscure can rise to the greatest heights by their sheer will and determination. But if one finds these examples credible, in many areas it is evident that we have indeed lost our moral compass. If it is by our actions that we are known, as a country, as reputable businessmen and women, it would appear that we are in some respects in pretty sad shape, far from living a life of virtue and concern for the greater good.

If we are not willing to return to MacIntyre's "Tradition" in order to reset our moral compass, where will we go? We run the risk of being "lost in space," just as in *The Rocky Horror Picture Show*: On the surface it is a lot of fun, but at our core we are operating with a life-damaging lack of values toward ourselves and our fellow man.

We are far less than what Maharishi called "the wise who are tools in the hands of the Divine, whose actions are for the welfare of the world." Our karma—the actions that bring upon us the consequences in our lives, both individually and as a society—is simply another way of saying, "As ye sow, so shall ye reap," and what is it indeed that we are sowing?

Our collective dharma is off course, and we need to do something to put ourselves back on the evolutionary path. Many of our actions both as individuals and as a society are less than evolutionary. Many of our actions would make us eligible kar-mically for the annual "Darwin Award," the spoof award given every year in recognition of the most non-evolutionary acts man can devise, acts which are putting *Homo sapiens* on the verge of extinction. One example is the guy who became famous, or perhaps infamous, for hovering above Los Angeles in his beach chair supported by helium balloons in the flight path of airplanes. Maybe finding a tradition to follow wouldn't be such a bad choice for us.

All is not lost, however, and again in the words of *The Rocky Horror Show*, we can take heart that there is "light in the dark-ness of everybody's life."

FOUR

PRIOR TO PLATO

....

He who is not established has no intellect,
nor has he any steady thought. The man without
steady thought has no peace; for one without peace
how can there be happiness?

MAHARISHI,
BHAGAVAD-GITA: A NEW TRANSLATION AND COMMENTARY
(Chapter II, Verse 66)

As a freshman at Vanderbilt in 1962, I convinced my advisor to let me take a Humanities Course, a summary course on the history, art, and philosophy of Western civilization. It was a course the university usually recommended for senior students, but I had spent a year in Europe as an exchange student, and I had gone to a rigorous prep school. I convinced them I was ready for it. Too bad. Little did I know of critical thinking. Little did I know of history, art, and philosophy. In retrospect, it would have been better to follow the usual curriculum and have had several years of college behind me before jumping into the entire history of Western civilization. I graduated from college with only a freshman's perspective on cultural history, and it was fascinating to me later to learn more of the ideas and cultures that had influenced the ancient Greeks, whose civilization had formed the beginning of my cultural journey. I discovered that the Vedic culture from which TM originates was a major influence on the Greeks.

Parallel with my comeuppance in college was the discovery of William Sargant's book *Battle for the Mind*. My religious underpinnings were shaken to the core from reading this book. Conversions happen outside the Church? Jonestown and the Kool-Aid poisonings of four hundred people actually happened? We could be manipulated by skillful "salesmen"? No wonder I was leery when I first heard about Maharishi and his TM technique. I attended three introductory lectures before I felt convinced—and not by anyone's charisma but by the scientific research on Transcendental Meditation—to learn TM. The research and the experience of others was the all-important link that tied me to the TM experience. By then I was down and out. I had left my family. I had left my Church, but I was not going to be duped. I was the

Existential wanderer, along with many of my friends. We had given up our ties to roots. By choice we had severed ties with our traditions, as so many young people do.

• • •

There is tremendous strength and appeal in tradition. We may have traveled far on our own. We may have experienced other thoughts and other cultures. We have certainly expanded our awareness of the world, but eventually we may choose to return home to what we know.

But where is that? *What* is that? Home? Home is now so altered by our moral relativism; so many suburbs and half thoughts have been built up around what used to be home, the compass has become so broken for many of us, that home will never be found. We are on our own, and we probably wouldn't even recognize home if we could find it.

Our Western civilization began with the Greeks—their thought, their gods, their culture—or so we were taught, so we have read. After all, we must begin somewhere. Limitations are necessary to keep us from dissolving into the boundless. Our minds and our ability to assimilate are finite. But if we have only a limited understanding of history, we live in a small box with small boundaries surrounded by darkness.

The French Enlightenment philosopher Voltaire (1694–1774), who voraciously studied and researched world cultures, wrote: "I am convinced that everything has come down to us from the banks of the river Ganges."

German philosopher Friedrich Schlegel, in his book *On the Language and Wisdom of India* (1808), came to the sweeping conclusion that "Everything, absolutely everything is of Indian origin."

In his extensively researched and illuminating book *India in Greece* (1852), Scottish scholar E. Pococke wrote of his analysis of Sanskrit terms that have been found in the Vedic literature and culture from India and carried over in their derivatives to other people and place names from Scandinavia to South America, from Greece to Ireland, and to the steppes of Russia. From his analysis he posits that long before the Greeks, Vedic civilization from India had reached the corners of the world. His deduction: "The whole of Greece from the era of the supposed Godships of Poseidon and Zeus down to the close of the Trojan war was Indian in language, sentiment, religion, peace, and war."

William Durant (1885–1981), historian, professor, author, and winner of the Pulitzer Prize in 1968 and the Presidential Medal of Freedom in 1977, researched and wrote an eleven-volume series, *The Story of Civilization*. Based on his research findings, he states a conclusion perhaps surprising to those of us whose education began only with the Greeks: "India was the motherland of our race, and Sanskrit the mother of Europe's languages. She was the mother of our philosophy...of our mathematics...of the ideals embodied in Christianity...of self-government and democracy. Mother India is in many ways the mother of us all."

And in his *History of the British Empire in India* (1841), Edward Thornton wrote: "When Greece and Italy, those cradles of European civilization, nursed only the tenants of the wilderness—India was the seat of wealth and grandeur."

To limit the origins of our cultural understanding to the Greeks is contrary to what we now know: Our Western culture and intellectual tradition has its roots in the culture and thought of India. Most of us are probably not ready to return to MacIntyre's Thomistic version of Catholicism to find solace in tradition. There is more to it than that.

In today's world of moral relativism, many of us tend to make our own traditions, find our own rituals, make our own rules—things that work for us. Ideas and directives imposed from the outside often have to be examined, decided, and if necessary re-worked to make them our own.

Professor Daniel Robinson, a member of the philosophy faculty at Oxford University and author or editor of more than forty books on moral, psychological, and legal philosophy and the history of the founding of the United States, makes the point that our forefathers came from Britain as good, loyal subjects of the king. They sought a better life and religious freedom, but still followed the dictates of the monarchy for over a century. As George III grew ever more tyrannical, and as we developed our own representative form of government, in self-defense we threw off the shackles of the monarchy and proceeded to reinvent ourselves as a country.

Professor Robinson cites one of the great political philosophers of the French Enlightenment, Montesquieu, who in his book *The Spirit of the Laws* (1748) makes the distinction between a monarchy, which governs based on the qualities of honor and obedience instilled in its subjects; a tyranny, which governs based on the fear it instills in its populace; and a democracy, whose enlightened, independent people are grounded in "Virtue"— self-knowledge and involvement in their government.

As the world becomes more democratized, no longer subject to the honor and obedience instilled by a monarch, or the fear imposed by a tyrant, we may reason that people look more to themselves for direction. We form new traditions to guide us, new laws to govern us, all to give us a self-directed sense of stability and security, of solace and certainty, and an organized moral society in which to live and to hand down to our children. We began our country as a religiously oriented society, but today one has only to look around to see that for many people this orientation has weakened, and for some it has disappeared altogether.

As we make our own directions, create our own moral fabric, and reinvent ourselves without directives imposed from the outside, we would be wise to make sure we have a life-supporting sense of values. We need a morality that will work for all people, not just one based on personal greed and self-centeredness, which both as individuals and as a society we can descend into with our complete freedom. But when, for some, even religion can be suspect, what do we do?

In 1957, British psychiatrist and researcher William Sargant's book *Battle for the Mind: A Physiology of Conversion and Brain-Washing* was published. Sargant was inspired by the research of Russian physiologist and Nobel Laureate Ivan Pavlov on behavioral changes in dogs repeatedly subjected to overwhelming stresses. Pavlov's dogs were nearly drowned in a flood of his laboratory, and he found their training and behavior suddenly and irreparably altered by the trauma. Sargant began his own research into what makes people change their minds.

Studying religious conversions, brainwashing techniques used on British POWs during World War II, native practices from New Guinea to the voodoo of Haiti, and the snake-handling cults in the Deep South in the USA, Sargant found a common thread: "If [in an individual] a complete sudden collapse can be produced by prolonging or intensifying emotional stress [often drumming, dancing, chanting], the cortical slate may be wiped clean temporarily of its more recently implanted patterns of behavior, perhaps allowing others to be substituted more easily."

Sargant was brought up as a Methodist in England and began studying how John Wesley, the founder of Methodism, produced conversions by working his congregations into a fervor of excitement, making them suggestible to the solution of conversion. He found that in this state the subject became open to whatever solution happened to be nearest in the group or society where he happened to be, hence the conversion.

As a young man, I experienced for myself how this common thread of emotional collapse still exists in the religious phenomena of conversion, of God's grace descending on us. It is held in Methodism (I remember from my Sunday school) that we are not capable of contacting God by ourselves alone. God contacts us. It is only through his "grace" that we are "saved." And I, for one, was typically open to finding the "religious fervor" through song, prayer, and preaching, in order to have the experience of

God's presence. I can tell you that when it happens, it is exciting. It is a wonderful emotional release, and it is not confined to Methodism. Most religions have their corresponding methods.

But this phenomenon of the suggestibility of the mind, in addition to opening us to the emotional catharsis that gives us the experience of the validity of our religious beliefs, can also misdirect us to false prophets and charismatic leaders who may or may not be operating with our personal interests in mind. As Sargant reveals to us from his research, under the right conditions we can become putty in the hands of a torturer, a tyrant, or a skilled manipulator.

This is not to denigrate the experience of a religious conversion at all. For those of us who have had this experience, we can attest to the fact that it provides us with quite possibly the greatest sense of unity that we have ever had. But we probably also know that it is impossible to live and function in this sense of euphoria on a daily basis. Gradually, over time, life has a way of getting in the way, and the feeling of euphoria dissipates. People are unkind. Life's problems still hit us square on, causing stress which makes it difficult to maintain the experience that seemed so real at church or in the quiet of our own room.

It was my experience that this sense of euphoria is by nature fleeting. And what tends to follow is perhaps a sense of respect and awe for what has happened, but also a sense of depression that we have lost it. Once we have had the experience of a conversion, our spirits and emotional well-being are subject to fluctuation depending on how close we feel to God at any given moment. Our religious practice becomes a way of keeping in touch with the vestiges of the wonderful sense of God's presence that we experienced in the conversion.

Sargant further recounts his experience with a group of anthropologists who studied indigenous tribes and their religions. He describes their experience, which he found to be similar to Wesley's conversion of the Methodists in the mid-1700s. The group participated in the dances and chanting of the tribe and experienced the cathartic rush, the "sense of God" produced by the euphoria induced by the dancing, the chanting, and the rhythmic drumbeat. Several of the anthropologists, feeling convinced that this religion was the one for them, converted at least temporarily to the religion of the tribes they were studying.

We have free choice, and we can choose from a panoply of religious and secular possibilities to satisfy our need for this sense of certainty, this sense of personal completion, this sense of unity. Or, fearing self-delusion and its consequences, we can simply deny the existence of a personal God and choose instead to live a totally secular life. Or, we can follow the dictates, the rules, and the ritual of the Catholic Church, the Protestant Church, or our temple or mosque. We may not be swept away in the euphoria of a sense of conversion, but we at least can take comfort in the substance, the sense of authority, and the certainty and tradition of these centuries-old institutions.

Many of us, in the spirit of Existentialism—where each individual is responsible for his or her own salvation, happiness, and well-being—explore and find our own way to unity and certainty based on what we know, what we learn, and what we find our reason and our intellect can accept. Our acceptance is then based on our feeling and rational analysis of what will be best for us. We continue the search until we find a tradition to which we can relate, one that is rational and reasonable, one that we find to be effective, one that can be proven to work, to bring positive values, truth, morality, positive direction, self-sufficiency, and happiness.

Understanding Sargant's research is important. We do not want to be duped, manipulated, or brainwashed in the search for our path. A conversion may be the way we find our path, but we may also want to make a rational decision as we explore the choices of which tradition to follow.

It is from the ancient Vedic tradition of India—the oldest continuous body of knowledge in the world—that Maharishi Mahesh

Yogi came in 1958, bringing a simple, natural meditation technique to the West. Meditation in India is recognized as a method of contacting one's inner being. The goal of the practice is inner peace, inner silence, and contact with an inner sense of unity and certainty, or as Maharishi terms it, "the Absolute."

Scholars and monks can argue that it takes more or less time—perhaps years of effort—to become proficient in one's practice of meditation. However, the Transcendental Meditation technique requires no extensive study, no physical or intellectual effort, and no long years of practice for one to become proficient. The experience of "transcending" in my experience was immediate. The scientific research verifies that Transcendental Meditation is unique. It is not a belief system based on faith or fervor. All that is required to practice Transcendental Meditation is a human nervous system. It does not produce a sense of euphoria based on excitement and conversion, but it reliably produces a sense of fullness and completeness.

The feeling of transcendence one experiences with Transcendental Meditation is not in danger of disappearing. It reappears each time we meditate, and the longer we do it, the more this experience of transcendence, this experience of unity, peace, and self-sufficiency carries over into the activity of our daily lives. It does this whether we are a Christian, a Jew, a Muslim, a Hindu, a Buddhist, or of any other religious persuasion. Even an agnostic or an atheist can have the experience of transcending.

Transcendental Meditation is based in a tradition that is thousands of years old. It does not require the asceticism of the monk, the recluse who drops out of society, to achieve union with God. It does not require giving up the normal life and routines of the householder who works in the world. It does not require any conversion or overwhelming emotional release whatsoever. Transcendental Meditation is simply a mental technique that produces deep rest, releases stress, and thereby enables us to perform more effective action so that we can fulfill our desires. For those

of us who have lived through the loss and uncertainty of euphoria, for those who have lived through the dark night of the soul,
and indeed for all of us, whatever our persuasion, Transcendental
Meditation can establish us in steadiness and peace at the deepest
level of our being.

FIVE

THE PURPOSE OF LIFE

....

Expansion of happiness is the purpose of life,
and evolution is the process through which it is fulfilled.
Life begins in a natural way, it evolves, and happiness expands.
The expansion of happiness carries with it the growth
of intelligence, power, creativity, and everything that
may be said to be of significance in life.

MAHARISHI,
SCIENCE OF BEING AND ART OF LIVING

Over the years, I have often marveled at the peace and happiness that descends on me from the practice of Transcendental Meditation. I have come to accept it. I no longer question it. In fact, I have come to expect it in a humble sort of way. It's not a miracle. Maharishi has told us to expect it, as stress is relieved from our lives. Roadblocks dissolve. Intuition expands. Our personal dharma becomes apparent to us. We learn to turn inward for the answers to our problems.

• • •

The expansion of happiness is not a hedonistic sort of thing. It is a natural outcome of transcending. But it was fascinating to me to read the Greek philosopher Aristotle's reasoning about happiness, for it parallels the knowledge from the Vedas, composed millennia earlier, that is embodied in Maharishi's technique of TM.

Writing in his *Nicomachean Ethics* in 350 BC, Aristotle made a reasoned argument that the final end of everything we do is to produce personal happiness, which he terms *eudaemonia*—a flourishing, virtuous life of right action and excellence. If we think about it, following Aristotle's line of reasoning, we realize that we plant the seed and tend the crop, not as an end in itself, but to grow food to eat. We eat, not as an end in itself, but so we can live and be healthy, and have an opportunity to seek our happiness. Similarly we study to have a career, not just as an end in itself, but in order to support ourselves and our families financially, with the anticipated end result of happiness for ourselves, our spouse, and our children.

In Aristotle's day, he used the example that bridlemakers made bridles not as an ultimate end, but to enable the soldier to guide the horse in order to win wars to accumulate more real estate, more wealth and power, all to produce more happiness for individuals. There is nothing we do in our life that has an end more important to us than our own personal happiness. Even helping others has as its goal—what? We do for others, but doing for others gives us a sense of well-being and personal happiness. Our happiness is quite simply the ultimate end in itself.

In Aristotle's words: "What is the highest of all goods achievable by action[?] Verbally there is very general agreement; for both the general run of men and people of superior refinement say that it is happiness." He arrives at this conclusion by pointing out that happiness is something we always choose for its own sake and never for the sake of anything else. We choose honor, pleasure, reason, and virtue for the sake of happiness. We do not choose happiness for the sake of honor, pleasure, or virtue, but only for itself. Happiness is the "ultimate good."

But there are roadblocks to happiness at every turn. As Arjuna, the hero of the *Bhagavad-Gita*, was incapacitated when confronted with a double bind—fight and defend your kingdom, for it is your duty as a warrior, but in the process you will kill your kinsmen whom you love—so are we presented with potentially incapacitating double binds. If I love *this* person, I cannot be with *that* person. If I complete this job, presentation, or project, it will be done and available for people to judge. But what if they judge it (and me) negatively? If I cheat on this business deal, I will be undermining my entire moral belief structure, but the money and the opportunities are so vast I feel I must cheat to win. We are torn. We want the easy way, the instant gratification, but none of us want to suffer the consequences. The virtuous life which leads to the flourishing of eudemonia—to our happiness— often escapes us.

Like Arjuna, confronted with our own conflicting choices, our own double binds, we can be rendered incapable of action, and often we throw down our quiver of arrows in despair. We set our bow aside to "think about it," unable to decide which path we should follow, or we act precipitously—rules be damned—and we suffer the consequences of our action. If we are lucky, we keep at least one of the lovers. If we are lucky, we muddle through to the end of our project and present it completed, as best we can. If we are lucky, we make the moral choice when confronted with the options that can produce enduring bad karma in our lives. We remember that "as we sow, so shall we reap," and we choose the path of virtue.

If we have made the choice not to live by the rules we have inherited—the rules of our religion, the rules of our monarchy, the rules of our dictator, or even the rules of our democratic society—if we rebel against the traditions of our parents, and our past, if we abandon our culture for a new paradigm, if we choose the life of moral relativism, where each of us makes his or her own rules, if we choose these paths, we live in a place fraught with danger, a place where we have little or no direction from the knowledge of the past, the millions of paths already tried and discarded, or the paths tried and succeeded in.

How will we know which course to follow if we are only self-directed? How can we be sure that we can trust our self, if our direction comes only from our self and our self is susceptible to greed, to self-deception, and to the fancy baubles of the moment? Our religions, our traditions, and our culture can be safe havens for us, providing direction to our lives, but many of us have cast them away. How do we know what direction we should follow, what is best for us if we don't follow a known path?

In the several years I spent teaching film production and film history in the mid-1970s, I used to show my students a short documentary film entitled *A Portrait of Brian Beavers,* in which a half-Indian, half-Scottish hermit living in the Pacific Northwest recounts his experience growing up with the Native Americans. Now stooped with age, bearded and disheveled, he lives in his log hut in the wilderness, surrounded by the deer and animals he feeds in the dirt yard outside his hut. He remembers, as a youth, watching the tribe's medicine man gather all the young boys in a line before him. Beavers describes how the medicine man blew a small dart into each boy with his blowgun, and the boy fell to the ground in a sort of fit. The medicine man would then reach down, feel the boy up and down, and at the end announce, "This boy will be a hunter, this boy will grow crops, and this boy will become an elder of the tribe," and so on. Each boy's duty and direction was determined by the tribe's wise man. That method apparently worked for Beaver's group of Native Americans. I think it only confounded my college students.

In our religious instruction, a child is often asked, "What do you want to be when you grow up? What is God calling you to do?" That can be a hard question when you are ten—it can still be a hard question when you are thirty, or fifty, or beyond! What is God calling you to do? What do you want to do? What is your *duty*? And how do you determine it? Listening can be a good place to start. Some of us pray about it, some of us listen to our elders and mentors. Eventually, some of us may learn the value of turning inward and asking ourselves, "What do I want? What do *I* want?" We learn the value of listening to ourselves. But can we really trust that?

Transcendental Meditation is a simple mental technique brought to us from an ancient and time-tested tradition. Practicing the technique as we have been taught, we settle down and reach a place of peace—a place of "self-referral." Gradually, with experience, we learn to trust this place within us; we learn to trust ourselves. We learn to listen to our inner voice, our intuition. The longer we meditate, the more aware of it we become. It is in this place deep inside ourselves that we find what we want to do. As a result of experiencing this place of self-referral and silence, our duty becomes apparent to us. It is as a result of experiencing this inner quietness that the teachings of our religion, our culture, and our traditions become even more understandable, even sweeter, and we can spontaneously and safely formulate our moral life.

While Transcendental Meditation is a technique for deep rest with extensive and corresponding health benefits, there is also a component of knowledge associated with the tradition from which it comes. One can simply enjoy the practice of meditating twice a day and the better health, improved relationships, and increased success in one's activities it brings. One can also choose to read and study the many books that have been written about Transcendental Meditation or view some of the thousands of hours of lectures given by Maharishi to further understand the process of meditation and the Vedic tradition of universal knowledge of life.

Whatever work or career path we choose, whatever religion, whatever philosophy, and whenever we make a choice, we by necessity limit ourselves. But that is all right, for without limitation, man's life dissolves in the boundless. Choice and limitations are an important part of life.

We can spend our lives pursuing the endless possibilities of knowledge and experience. Research just one subject and we begin to understand how little we know of the virtually unlimited possibilities for study. Choose one sport, and we begin to understand the essence of sport and the endless possibilities open to us. Choose one career path, and we focus our time and energy primarily in that direction. It is necessary that we do that. We choose a mate, a place to live, work to do, and ideas to believe in to follow life's course. We cannot follow all paths at once. Life by its nature involves choice, the exclusion of one thing for another. As Maharishi points out, we live our lives in the "relative," and it is in the relative world that we satisfy our basic necessities, for food, shelter, clothing, companionship, and love.

It is in our nature to seek more and more of what we want— more and fancier foods, bigger and fancier houses, finer clothes, more friends, more love, more knowledge, and more success. Our happiness often depends on whether we are successful in procuring more and more of these things in the relative. It is growth if we land a better job. It is growth if we find a breakthrough in our area of research, read a great book or an inspiring poem, or listen to a moving piece of music. It is inspiring and brings us happiness to look at a work of art which gives us the "aha" experience of yes, that is right, that is true, that is beautiful, and for a while we are satisfied. But satisfaction is fleeting. It lasts only for a time, and then we move on in our quest for more.

Personal satisfaction lies hidden away. We can pray for it. We can pine for it. We can search and listen for it, and we can find it. We can find it in the silence within us accessible through this technique of meditation. Instead of venturing outside of ourselves to find complete satisfaction, we can make the choice to venture into ourselves to find it. This turning in is not an avoidance of all the wonderful things of the world; it is not a negation or denial of the pleasures, the projects, the wealth, and accomplishments of the world. It is more like the directive on the airplane: "Put on your own oxygen mask before assisting others." First you turn within yourself to experience the expansive sense of yourself and then turn outward to experience all that is around you. We are simply able to function more effectively once we have an adequate supply of oxygen.

Just as we cannot will ourselves to be happy, to be in love, or to be wealthy, so we cannot will the experience of complete and lasting satisfaction. All of these experiences happen because we do our best to set up the environment and circumstances that will create and bring us love, wealth, and happiness. Then we can only wait and hope that it comes. Similarly, through the practice of Transcendental Meditation, we can set up an environment and circumstances that will create the experience of self-knowledge, of contentment, of unity, or as Maharishi terms it, "the Absolute." We can directly experience "the home of all the laws of Nature," and over time this experience of transcendence becomes the basis for achieving the wealth, love, and happiness that we seek in the relative.

Maharishi tells us, "Expansion of happiness is the purpose

of life, and evolution is the process through which it is fulfilled."
We can speed our evolution and our road to happiness by learning this simple mental technique, which will take us within in a
reliable manner and set up the environment within ourselves for
love, wealth, and happiness. It will enable us to intuit our duty
in life—our dharma—and then, just as the mask falls from the
ceiling of the airplane when there is a lack of oxygen, we can
reach up, pull it to us, and breathe deeply. We can experience for
ourselves that the purpose of life is the expansion of happiness. It
is not something ephemeral. It is a real experience that grows in
us the longer we practice Transcendental Meditation.

In Maharishi's commentary on the *Bhagavad-Gita* (Chapter
II, verse 41), he says: "The minds of those who do not practice
this Yoga are constantly in the field of sensory experience. This
fails to provide the mind with that great joy which alone can satisfy its thirst for happiness. That is why the minds of such people
continue to search and wander endlessly."

After being instructed in the Transcendental Meditation
technique and having their first experience transcending, forty
Tibetan Buddhist monks, still maintaining their Buddhist practices but now adding TM, told their TM teacher: "This is what
we have been looking for!"

A psychiatrist friend of mine, himself deep in depression at the
time, learned to meditate with TM. When a mutual friend asked
him to compare Transcendental Meditation to the Buddhist meditations he had been practicing for forty years, he said simply, "TM
is more direct." He's still a Buddhist, but he now practices the
TM technique twice daily as well. It took only a few days of this
meditation to neutralize his depression, and I have watched with
delight as his happiness grows and he regains his productivity.

SIX

THE PRACTICE OF
TRANSCENDENTAL MEDITATION

....

This is the technique of instantaneous realization.

MAHARISHI,
BHAGAVAD-GITA: A NEW TRANSLATION AND COMMENTARY
(Chapter II, Verse 45)

In 1990, my wife left for five months to attend a teacher training course at a major TM Center in Huntsville, Canada. We had made this decision together: She would study to become a teacher of Transcendental Meditation, and I would provide the financial support she would need as a full-time teacher. Having memorized entire bodies of knowledge relating to the instruction of TM, she completed the Huntsville course and went on to take additional instruction in Spain, after which she went to Holland to be with Maharishi for a time at his worldwide center. She came home a full-time teacher of Transcendental Meditation and over the years has instructed hundreds of people in the TM technique.

• • •

Why can't you just learn to meditate from a book? Why do you have to have a teacher?

To be effective, Transcendental Meditation must be properly taught by a trained teacher. Becoming certified as a teacher of Transcendental Meditation requires that one undergo a rigorous training procedure established directly by Maharishi. The process of meditating with TM is subtle. Without a teacher to guide the way, we may at first miss what is truly going on inside us when we transcend. We may dismiss it as just a feeling of the moment and fail to recognize the power and strength that flow so subtly into us from the process of meditating. —The effectiveness of the procedure may be distorted and lost—indeed, the process of transcending might not even take place.

It may seem strange, but every TM teacher says the same words during the instruction. Each teacher has his own personality and his own strengths, but the TM instruction they give is absolutely the same for everyone who learns. It was Maharishi's goal to "multiply himself," and he did it by training thousands of men and women as teachers of Transcendental Meditation, who then train each of us individually in the TM technique. Maharishi's method maintains the purity of the knowledge, and the purity is important. This is not a technique that a teacher may alter. It is a technique handed down for thousands of years, and every teacher of TM respects that tradition.

After explaining that TM is an effortless meditation technique and after performing a brief ceremony of gratitude to the tradition from which this teaching comes, a TM teacher will personally instruct you in how to meditate. As you learn to practice Transcendental Meditation properly, you will go beyond or "transcend" the ordinary surface level of the thinking process. You may experience a sense of unity—a sense of "instantaneous realization"—that will refresh and please you, something that you will want to return to regularly, and will return to regularly with your practice.

Transcendental Meditation is more powerful than we may at first realize. It does not involve physical activity. It is a mental process. We do not do it for the experience during the meditation, although this can be pleasant. Rather, we do it for the benefits of clearer thought, better health, a happier life—all the positive benefits that we receive in activity. It is a powerful process, and it is important that one practice it within the boundaries given by Maharishi and given through the trained teacher to us, the limitations and boundaries that have been tested and tried over millennia and handed down to us from the tradition of Vedic knowledge through Maharishi. Too much meditation may not be good for us; too little can be ineffective in producing the results we seek.

What happens when we practice Transcendental Meditation? Unlike some other forms of meditation, we are not directed to control our thoughts or focus on anything in particular. We are not seeking a destination. We are not seeking a specific experience.

We simply follow the instructions our teacher gives us for effort-less meditation and then "take it as it comes." The power in TM is that it is an effortless mental technique that gives us tremendous results.

In our instruction we learn that the important thing is that there is no judgment involved. It is important that we approach TM innocently. We do not try to meditate. We do it easily and naturally. If we let effort take over, if we try to meditate, then we destroy the simplicity and effectiveness of the process. We do not focus on or worry about what takes place in meditation. We simply perform the procedure as given to us during our per-sonal instruction. Learning TM is a safe and effective technique for self-development. You will be in good hands learning from a trained teacher.

Once you choose to learn, the teacher will take you through a seven-step process of instruction: Step 1—The Introductory Lecture, in which you will learn the basic principles and hear about the benefits that result from practicing TM. Step 2—The Preparatory Lecture, in which a teacher will go into greater detail about the mechanics of meditation and its history. Other people may attend the first two steps with you. Step 3—The Personal Interview, in which you will complete an interview form, be informed about the fee (yes, there is a fee to learn TM), and then schedule the day and time of your personal instruction.

Steps 4–7 take place on four consecutive days and involve a commitment of about an hour and a half each day. Step 4 is the Personal Instruction in TM, which takes place privately. It begins with a ceremony of gratitude to the tradition of masters from which this meditation comes, followed by the actual instruction. Your teacher will instruct you in how to meditate correctly for twenty minutes twice a day.

Steps 5–7 are three more sessions with the teacher—and often with a group of others who have learned on the same day—during which you discuss your experiences and receive more knowledge about the practice in each session.

Transcendental Meditation is simply a technique. It does not require that one have faith for it to work. It does not involve any sense of religious fervor for it to be effective. It is more like going to the gym to build our strength. We do not have to believe that exercise will make us stronger. We simply do it and gradually experience that we are able to stand straighter, lift heavier loads, and undertake more rigorous activity without tiring as we did before.

Since Transcendental Meditation is simply a technique, it does not conflict with our religious beliefs. We do not change our religion because we have learned to drive. We simply enjoy driving as a way to get us where we want to go faster than we could by walking. We can enjoy thinking about our religion while we drive, and we can enjoy the fellowship and ritual and peacefulness of our religion once we have driven to our place of worship. Driving is simply a means to get us there.

And because Transcendental Meditation is simply a technique, it does not require a change in our beliefs. We will notice changes in our life and benefits from the practice, but these will happen spontaneously from within us. They are not willed or reasoned into being by our own force and effort. They are not imposed from the outside by some higher authority. We simply meditate; perform our daily activity as usual, and any changes that happen to us happen spontaneously.

Once one has learned Transcendental Meditation, it is important to practice it twice a day according to the instructions we have received. We do not get stronger by simply thinking about exercise. We have to do it. We do not arrive at where we want to go by simply thinking about the location. We have to get in the car and drive to our location.

There will come a point in our lives when we choose not to confuse ourselves with dozens of beliefs and philosophies. We find a system that works for us, that produces the most energy, productivity, and happiness in our life; and we tend to stick to it. Most people who begin Transcendental Meditation find that this is the system that works for them.

What is it you have learned when you learned Transcendental Meditation? There are many forms of meditation, but if some-one gave you a technique of meditating that said, "Do not think about a monkey," what would you think about? You would not be able to get that monkey out of your mind. That monkey—don't think about it. Absolutely do not think about that monkey. It is important that you clear your mind of that monkey. Your life depends on it, but by being given the instruction to not think about it, instead it fills your mind. TM is not like that.

Stop thinking about your monkey—but think instead about a palm tree. Think of it swaying in the wind in the sand at the edge of the sea. The water is blue, and the waves lap at the seashore. Enjoy being there with your palm tree. Ah! Is that a monkey again in the top of the palm tree? It looks like him. He is hiding up there. Oh, but the palm fronds are beautiful. Think about the palm tree and feel it swaying in the breeze...feel it swaying... feel it swaying...the water...the palm tree...oh God, that monkey again!

And so it goes. Do not think about our suffering—we focus on it. Do not think about our problems at work—we focus on them. Do not think about the quarrel, or the love lost—we focus on them. The harder we try to clear our mind of them, the more they occupy our thoughts. Forcing our mind into mindfulness keeps our consciousness on the surface of thought and inhibits the transcending that is the source of the stress release and the benefits so many people experience with the practice of TM.

Maharishi speaks of "the principle of the second element." If we walk into a room that is dark, we do not worry and scheme and focus on the darkness in order to bring light into the room. We walk over to the wall switch and flip it on. The light then shines in the room and changes our focus immediately from the problem of the darkness in the room to the task at hand—whatever it is we came into the room to do. Instead of spending time worrying about how dark the room is, we have turned on the light switch and are able to go about our business and begin to be productive. This is the principle of the second element.

With the practice of Transcendental Meditation, we replace the darkness with the light, our stress with the experience of peace and vitality.

If we spend time focusing on what we lack, what we want to escape, we merely reinforce it in our mind. That monkey will simply not go away. By effortlessly allowing the mind to settle to deeper, more charming levels of the thinking process, which is what happens during the practice of Transcendental Meditation, the effect is a release from the superficial mental activity that occupies every waking moment, the mental activity that we use as a tool to solve all our problems, to control our activity, our direction, that tool which gives us the experience of who we are—or so we think.

The experience of the mind sinking to finer levels of the thinking process in Transcendental Meditation becomes that palm tree moving in the breeze. We become totally enamored with its charm, its beauty, its effortlessness, and the effect is that we lose the monkey, the darkness, and the stress of controlling our thoughts. We let go of controlling our mental activity, and in the resulting silence we descend into a peaceful, restful inner space, into a state of expanded awareness. We transcend thought and reach what Maharishi terms a state of "restful alertness—the source of thought." It is predictable. It is reproducible. It happens when we meditate with Transcendental Meditation, and it is this letting go and transcending that gives us the experience of who we really are. In meditating with TM, we let go of the mental activity, the control, the tools we typically rely on for our sense of well-being and identity. We experience that we are more than all the verbiage in our head.

We don't focus on the experiences we are having when we meditate; we simply follow our instructions for the performance of the technique and let go. We experience the fact that *we are not our thoughts*. Our life energy is based *not in our thoughts but in our silence*. And invariably we can reenter that silence again and again when we meditate with Transcendental Meditation. The silence is there for us, independent of fervor, independent of belief, independent of effort, dependent only on this effortless technique.

You will experience silence and deep rest when you practice TM, and you will experience the clear thinking and dynamic activity that result from this silence and deep rest when you come out of meditation into your daily life.

Indeed, in Maharishi's words: "This is the technique for instantaneous realization."

SEVEN

TWO PATHS

....

*There are in this world two paths: the Yoga of knowledge for
men of contemplation and the Yoga of action for men of action.*

MAHARISHI,
BHAGAVAD-GITA: A NEW TRANSLATION AND COMMENTARY
(Chapter III, Verse 3)

My father learned to fly Piper Cubs at Cornell ROTC prior to World War II. He built two different experimental planes when I was growing up, and was a member of the Experimental Aircraft Association. As a boy, I once flew with him in his Cessna 172 from Nashville to Ithaca. I can't say I wasn't scared flying at 10,000 feet in a bumpy little aircraft passing right over the center of Pittsburgh, but he loved it. I found that I preferred sailing, and as a teenager I built my own sailboat with the plans out of *Boys' Life*. Sailing was on terra firma, or at least closer to it than flying through the air. As an adult I sailed a Hobie Cat on our lake and took it to the ocean in North Carolina and sailed off the beach through the surf. Today my wife and I sail our 42-foot classic wooden yawl on the coast of Maine.

For me, sailing and flying are both accurate metaphors for life. Both require total attention to detail, and both require perfection of a technique. When my children were growing up, I used to tell them that every cotter pin, every O-ring had to be in place on the Hobie Cat, or we didn't go sailing that day. But have every detail on the boat exact, set the sails according to the wind, distribute your weight perfectly to keep the boat in balance, and you will be able to ride out the roughest seas. Perfect balance, everything in its place, and—sailing or flying—you can go like the wind. Get out of balance and every move is a struggle.

• • •

According to the Vedic tradition, as set forth in the *Bhagavad-Gita*, there are two paths to fulfillment in life—that of the householder, and that of the recluse. The householder includes most of us, living a life of action in society, work, and family. We have our aspirations, our loves, our desires, and through meditation we can access the source of power, contentment, and spontaneous right action that leads to fulfillment in our life of activity.

The recluse, on the other hand, leads a life of contemplation, prayer, and seclusion from society. Through worship, knowledge, and meditation, recluses are following their personal course of action that leads to fulfillment.

Maharishi counsels us that if householders try to live the life of a recluse—separate from their action, trying perhaps to "think about the spiritual life" as they go about their daily work—it leads to a division in their mind, a lack of focus, and a corresponding ineffectiveness in their life and activity. Neither should the recluse lose himself in the physical work of the householder, but rather continue on his own chosen path of contemplation and separation from society.

We can lose ourselves on the surface of ideas and feelings. It is so charming up here on the surface, so seductive with its ideas and sensations—the touching, the feeling, the loving. This is the part of life where success and failures are experienced, the area of life where pain and suffering are experienced. We may think we do not want to leave living life "on the edge." It is so exciting, so exhilarating, so satisfying, and at times so absolutely painful that we can hardly stand it, but we tell ourselves that it is worth it. We may tell ourselves that we have to live on the edge to achieve, to feel that we are alive. Anything less would not be being true to our self. We think this. We take courses. We educate ourselves, achieve at our jobs, fall in love and raise our families. It is the life of the householder. It is life in the relative—the life of action, life on the surface.

But there is more to it. Turn off the TV. Put down the drink. Meditate. Just as you feed yourself with wholesome food to gain strength and vitality, feed yourself with meditation. Feed yourself first. Then act. Gain strength from your inner resources, and then you can feed the world. Slow down to speed up.

As householders, our job is to live in the world. We cannot

disappear into the life of the hermit, the monk, the recluse who spends his time and energy in silence and spiritual development. And yet, this is the problem. We must take time to slow down and rest. We must take time to recharge ourselves. It would be wise for us to find a technique for spiritual development, one that is compatible with our life of activity. If we do not, we face total breakdown. At some point we will simply fall short and fail. We cannot demand so much of ourselves, yet we must, for we sense that our actions create who we are. It is by our actions that we are known, and life is short! There is not much time!

It is healthy to follow that need to *create ourselves*. It is necessary to achieve all we can.

As householders, we should not try to create a "mood of spirituality" while we work. Maharishi says it is this that has caused the state of ineffectiveness in Indian society. While we work, we need to focus on our work. This division—trying to create a mood of spirituality while performing our work—interferes with effective action. We work when we work; we meditate when we meditate. We avoid the mood making.

The Vedic tradition tells us that there are two paths in life—the Yoga of knowledge and contemplation (*Gyana Yoga*) for the recluse, and the Yoga of action (*Karma Yoga*) for the householder. Yet these two paths are not mutually exclusive. Both forms of Yoga require action. Recluses perform action by study and worship. Householders perform action by performing their work—their daily activity. By introducing Transcendental Meditation into each of their lives twice daily, both the householder and the recluse experience the deep rest that comes from the meditation and the resulting dynamic activity that leads to success in the path they have chosen.

After learning TM, the forty Buddhist monks mentioned above stated in wonder: "This is what we have been looking for." This was the transcending they had been seeking on the surface by focusing on giving up desire, focusing on nothingness. Instead they relaxed. They practiced Transcendental Meditation as they had been taught, and simply transcended.

Focusing is the monkey. The more we try to focus in meditation, the less we experience what it is we came here for. Our mind remains captured on the surface. We are too busy trying to get what we want and to avoid what we don't want. Until we learn to meditate in this unique way that Maharishi introduced from his experience with his master, we simply do not have the technique for *transcending*, and our minds will remain on the surface. We can achieve God's grace in a moment of fervor and excitement. We can experience the pleasure and excitement of solving a complex equation or scientific experiment. We can dissolve in the bliss of a loving moment with another, but it all passes quickly and our mind returns to the surface—refreshed perhaps, but searching again and again for the state of unity we momentarily gained.

During one of his talks to a group of college students at Humboldt State College in California in the early 1970s, Maharishi was asked by students about chanting as a way to transcend. He replied that one can chant and chant until one reaches a state of exhaustion, but this only clears the mind through exhaustion, not by transcending to the source of thought. It does not give the renewed energy and vitality one finds in Transcendental Meditation; it merely tires one out.

Maharishi points out that a muddle has been created in this path to realization. If the householder tries to live the solitary life of the Yoga of knowledge and contemplation, he or she becomes less practical and effective in their work. Similarly, if the recluse tries to live the active life of the householder, the Yoga of action, he loses his skill of impartial discrimination and contemplation. Both paths are equally valid for developing a full life. The path we choose should be the one that suits our natural tendencies.

How then does the householder, totally focused on performing the action of his daily life, develop the spiritual side of life? How does a person working in the world achieve *self-realization*?

There are two aspects of life—the relative and the Absolute. It is the experience of meditating that ties them together. By contacting the Absolute in the silence of our meditation, our actions in the relative, where we live every day, become more effective.

In his commentary on the *Bhagavad-Gita*, in Chapter III, Verse 1, Maharishi points out that, "The relative aspect [of life] is perishable and the absolute is imperishable. In order to give meaning to life, it is first necessary to bring the perishable aspect into living harmony with the imperishable. This is achieved through action according to one's dharma, which maintains existence in a way that furthers one's own evolution and that of others. In order to set the whole stream of life flowing naturally in the ascending current of dharma, it is necessary to cultivate the resolute intellect."

In other words, to perform our work in a thorough and effective manner to the best of our ability, whether we are a recluse or a householder, we need the clarity and focus that result from diving within to the Absolute in our practice of Transcendental Meditation. We need to learn a technique that will give us the results we seek. How do we do this?

Picture yourself for a moment sitting on the runway in the cockpit of a small airplane. You are by yourself—a "recluse" in the plane. The instrument panel and controls are neatly and ergonomically laid out before you and around you. Your job is to take this plane up into the air, circle the airport, and land it safely. You have no training. Perhaps you have flown before, but only as a passenger; someone else has always been at the controls. You must get this plane off the ground, fly up and circle the airport, and land safely. You feel your life depends on it. Yet you know nothing about the controls, nothing about the technique of flying. What do you do?

Fortunately, you see a trained instructor jogging toward you across the tarmac. He climbs into the passenger seat next to you and introduces himself as an experienced pilot who is here to teach you. The pilot smiles broadly and begins explaining each of the controls and dials. You gradually begin to understand the meaning and function of everything around you. Each explanation is a revelation and adds to your understanding. It doesn't take long before you have the knowledge and the confidence to grab the joy stick, taxi down the runway, soar into the air, bank and turn as you circle the airport, and with the coaching and assistance of the experienced pilot, bring your craft back to a safe landing on the runway. You feel elated. You thank your instructor, and you are prepared for your next flight with the instructor by your side, and your next, until you eventually solo, and you are on your own. You have learned to fly.

Sitting in that cockpit alone prior to instruction is life before you have learned the technique. You can experiment. You can fumble with the switches and pedals. You can accelerate and then lose confidence. You can try again and again, but do you really want to try to take off not knowing how fast you need to go to safely launch the airplane off the ground, much less circle the airport? It is frightening. You can ask some of the staff back in the hangar what each switch and pedal do. But it is a time-consuming and inefficient way to learn what you need to know to be able to fly safely.

Your instructor teaches you. The "relative," the confusion of the unknown you first experienced sitting there in the cockpit, gives way to the warm glow of confidence and joy as you master the technique and soar into the air. Looking down on the fields and town, you realize it is the knowledge imparted to you by your instructor that has enabled you to experience the sheer and absolute joy of flying, and now you can do it all alone—a "recluse" in the sky.

Now imagine yourself on your favorite body of water, sitting in a sailboat. At the moment, there is no wind. The water is dead calm. You enjoy the sunshine, the warmth. The varnished wood trim on the boat gleams in the sun. The white sails overhead reach into the sky. Life is good. You feel a breath of wind, and the sails begin to flutter. You are not sure what to do. There are all these ropes on the boat—these lines all over the place. Should you pull on one? The sails are flapping now, and you sit there not knowing what to do to make this thing move. The flapping sails are beginning to annoy you. Your lack of knowledge is an impediment to action. You begin to feel a bit stupid. You see the other sailboats around you moving. The people on board are smiling and obviously enjoying sailing. Not you. You don't know how.

Fortunately, next to you in the cockpit sits an experienced sailor who is there to teach you. The experienced sailor smiles and begins explaining each of the features of the boat. He shows you how to pull in the "main sheet," that rope lying on the floor of the cockpit. As you pull it in, the sail begins to tighten and fill, and the boat begins to move. Your sailing instructor tells you to place your hand on the "tiller"—that stick at the back of the boat—and he tells you to pull it slightly toward you. The boat "heads off" a bit and begins to "heel" over—to tilt from the wind in the sails. It is a new experience. It is pleasant.

You gradually realize that you are not in danger even though the boat is heeling and picking up speed. You are in control. The sense of exhilaration as you move through the water powered only by the wind is a rush for you. This is great. The balance comes quickly, and your instructor gives you advice about improving the trim of the sails as the wind picks up and you go even faster. Soon you are flying across the water—still in control, still in balance—and you are on the verge of ecstasy as you experiment more and more and refine your technique. Now that you have been taught by your instructor, you know you can do this yourself. You can sail. You have learned the technique.

This is your path now. You are ready for the races, ready to graduate to the bigger boats. You walk over to the yachts at the dock. They are swarming with people, all preparing for the next race. Where do you fit in? It's up to you now. You have to find your place on a crew. You have to learn to grind the winches, or take the role of bowman handling the spinnaker. Or will you be the navigator, the helmsman, or just rail meat hanging over the side as the boat heels? Where do you fit into the active society of the racing set?

You've learned the technique, the basic principles of sailing, and you watch. You focus and hone your skills. Gradually the crew realizes you are capable and strong. They put you to work. You become part of the team. You start to fit into this esoteric society of sailors, of "householders" racing their way through life. You know the basics. You refine your technique, and you realize that everything you do on this yacht relates to the basic principles you learned from your sailing instructor: set the course, trim the sails, everything in perfect balance, and—small boat or mega-yacht—you will fly through the water and the waves, you will ride out the heaviest winds, you will race the course, or cruise to unknown destinations, safe and secure in your experience. You know how to sail.

Flying and sailing are both wonderful metaphors for how to live our life. Learn the technique, learn the procedures, pay attention, practice them, perfect them, then set the ailerons, trim the sails, maintain your sense of balance, and you can fly forward at great speeds. When you are tired, rest. Once you are rested, resume action. And to achieve the greatest speed, you cannot be off daydreaming about something else. You must pay attention or run the risk of crashing or capsizing.

Whether you choose to fly alone in a small plane or to sail on a yacht with a crew to get to your destination, you have learned techniques for moving through time and space. The techniques produce bliss and satisfaction. Both have their own appeal. Whether you are alone in your private plane or fitting into the well-managed structure of a racing crew, you have your technique, the principles of balance, the inner certainty and confidence that you know what you are doing. The only limitation to keep in mind is that you don't try to pile a passel of friends into your small Piper Cub, and neither do you drop out and try to live a withdrawn and solitary life when you have chosen to contribute to the success of a racing crew.

Whichever path you choose, you realize your teacher has taught you well. You have mastered the skill, and the technique is now your own. You choose whether you will follow one path or the other. Both are valid. Both get you to a place of bliss, satisfaction, and happiness, but you make your choice and go with it. You do not try to be a recluse and a man of action at the same time. They are two distinct paths for reaching your destination.

EIGHT

MOUNT ATHOS

....

*Those interested in spiritual progress have for centuries
adopted an outlook suited only to the recluse way of life.
While perfectly valid for the few who retire from the world,
such an outlook has no place in the lives of the vast majority
of mankind who lead the householder's way of life.*

MAHARISHI,
BHAGAVAD-GITA: A NEW TRANSLATION AND COMMENTARY
(Chapter III, Verse 3)

In northern Greece, a forty-mile-long peninsula stretches far into the Aegean Sea, named after the tall mountain that graces its summit: Mount Athos. Mount Athos is home to twenty monasteries built between AD 985 and AD 1500. Athos also contains numerous smaller communities, or *sketes*, housing only a few monks who are artisans, gardeners, silversmiths, and painters of the beautiful icons for which Mount Athos is so renowned. Those monks who wish to live a completely solitary life devoted only to prayer and meditation live as total recluses in huts interspersed in the surrounding hills, fed by devoted brothers who bring them food. To minimize worldly temptation for the monks, no women are allowed to visit Mount Athos, and there are no female animals.

The first monastery, Philotheou, was built at the end of the tenth century. Nineteen others followed over the next five centuries. Athos is a living museum, housing vast libraries of illuminated texts, gold-framed icons of the Virgin Mary and other saints, treasures given by kings and princes of the Russian and Byzantine empires.

• • •

In 1974, I served as part of a small film crew from the United States, funded by a grant from the National Endowment for the Humanities. We had received permission to film the first documentary ever made of Mount Athos's disappearing lifestyle. What in the Middle Ages had been a society of ten thousand monks has been reduced to no more than five hundred souls in all the monasteries, but the lure of Athos lingers on. The monasteries of Athos draw devout pilgrims of the Greek Orthodox faith as well as the simply curious, who, having obtained a permit from the government of Athos, can hike the dirt roads and dusty paths over the mountains connecting the monasteries. Most travelers take the simpler route and visit by caïque, a small motorboat that delivers mail, supplies, and passengers along the coast of the peninsula.

Our film crew had the opportunity to view and photograph the magnificent monasteries, some perched on cliffs with views of the Aegean. We filmed the treasures and the libraries, the icons and the illuminated manuscripts, even the monks at work, at prayer, and at their meals. We filmed in the chapels—magnificent celebrations with gold vestments and prescribed ritual and chanting of the psalms.

Athos is a bastion of tradition. Nothing in their ritual, their beliefs, has changed for centuries. Our job was to capture the highlights of this life from the past before it disappears entirely.

The coordinator of our project was Greek. He understood what the Greek Orthodox audience would want to see—the icons and wealth of Athos in the context of the monasteries and their perches along the sea. For the uninitiated among us, however, the burning question was: What were they doing there? Why had these men left their lives in active society? Why were they living a life grounded in the religion of the Middle Ages? What motivated them?

We found our answer in Father John. Father John was in his eighties. He had a flowing white beard and was dressed in black robes. At an early age he had emigrated from Greece to Chicago, where he worked as a restaurateur. His dream had been to return to Greece and become a monk on Mount Athos, which he did upon his retirement from the restaurant business. Father John spoke perfect English, one of the few monks who did, and he agreed to be interviewed on film.

With camera and tape recorder running, I sat on the steps of the monastery holding the microphone while Father John told us his history of moving to the United States as a young man and his long-planned-for return to the spiritual center of Athos. He talked about the history of the monasteries, but then he gave us the following description about the life of a monk on Mount Athos:

The life of a monk is hard.

We work eight hours a day.

We pray eight hours a day.

We rest eight hours a day.

We pray for the safety and security of the world...

Sitting on the steps with him, hearing his history and his devotion, one had to be impressed by the discipline evidenced in the life of a monk on Mount Athos, and then he added:

A monk must fight three evils.

The first is ourselves.

The second is the world.

The third is the devil.

And he is the enemy of us all...

Mount Athos made a huge impression on me. At the time, we simply recorded what Father John said. But years later, after learning Transcendental Meditation and reflecting on what Father John had described as the continual fight against three evils, I realized how sad, and how unnecessary, this negative view of the world is.

• • •

The three evils? Ourselves? The world? The devil? We had made a documentary film to capture the monks' lives, their treasures, and their traditions, not to judge what they held as beliefs. But I found it fascinating that a man would leave the world to attempt to find salvation in what appeared to me to be a continual struggle that could only alienate one from the all-important realization of Self. Here the Self was insignificant. It was to be battled with. Evil was rampant in their view of the world. And the devil was to be fought and if possible subdued. For me, this was the antithesis of the life in happiness that I had come to experience with my practice of Transcendental Meditation.

While it was impossible not to be humbled by the splendor of Mount Athos—the wealth of the cathedrals, the libraries of the monasteries, and the commitment and devotion of the monks—to understand it, one must put the monastic life into the context of the recluse. These men are following their dharma. They have made a choice to drop out of the world and pursue enlightenment according to the dictates of their religion. They are sincere in their prayers for the safety and security of the world. They seek personal enlightenment and redemption, and they do it, at least according to Father John, by daily battle with their three evils—hoping and praying that God will help them win.

I can reflect back now on Mount Athos with a better understanding of the distinction between the life of the recluse and the life of the householder. Perhaps one cannot really understand the other, but for the householder, in my experience, if we focus continually on the negative, on battling the three evils—what will we get? If we choose to focus on these "monkeys," they will control our lives and thoughts. We can make our choice to live a life of constant battle, or we can switch on the light in the room and focus on the pursuit of happiness. It is our choice.

The questioning and scientific reasoning begun by Sir Francis Bacon in the early 1600s was further developed by Copernicus, Galileo, Kepler, Newton, Descartes, Voltaire, and many other scientists and philosophers during the seventeenth and eighteenth centuries. It was found by the thinking man that we need not be guided by the dogma, the restrictions, of a controlling religion. But here on Mount Athos was a perfectly preserved Byzantine museum of the Greek Orthodox Church. One could say, superficially perhaps, that the light of reason had never been turned on here.

Even monks, both Christian and Buddhist, have found that Transcendental Meditation is a way of liberation and fulfillment of personal seeking. Adopt it, experience the self-realization that results from its practice, and it can bring fulfillment even to the practice of one's religion. We can choose the good things—the values, the strength of working in a group, the morality, the love and fellowship, even the redemption that we find in our religion.

Through practicing the technique of Transcendental Meditation, we can experience daily the Absolute, the true essence of what it is we seek in our religion. We can bring the "perishable aspect into living harmony with the imperishable." And we can experience for ourselves that we are meant to be happy.

As householders, we can learn Transcendental Meditation and no longer be a Sunday Christian, or Saturday Jew, or a practitioner of any other religion one day a week. Instead, we can live life-supporting values spontaneously, daily, moment by moment. We can discover our dharma, our duty in life, and work it with all our heart. There is no need to be distracted and divided by worrying about the three evils, nor by our guilt and shame. Instead, we can meditate twenty minutes, twice a day, and reach the state of total rest and rejuvenation from which we emerge refreshed and ready for work, for love, for activity. Through the practice of TM we will find our religion to be even more meaningful and fulfilling.

As a young man, before ever hearing about Transcendental Meditation, I arrived at the conclusion that it was imperative that I strive to be where I was when I was there and to do what I was doing when I was doing it. I didn't always succeed, but it was a way to help me achieve a sort of personal authenticity.

Whether you are an actor creating a character, an engineer designing refrigerator handles or the bridge over the river, or a parent putting the stroller in the back of the car, if you are aware—if you are where you are when you are there, and doing what you are doing when you are doing it—you will be centered. You will be drawing on the balance and creative energy that flows from your Self, from your very center. But how to maintain this state? Before learning Transcendental Meditation, I found it to be elusive and impossible to will this state of mind continually into being.

But after learning Transcendental Meditation, I found that my meditation practice gave me the experience of inner silence, an inner expansion into a seemingly limitless source of energy, twice a day transcending to the source of thought, pure consciousness, the Absolute. It has enabled me to be where I am when I am there and do what I am doing when I am doing it, spontaneously—automatically. Meditate with TM and you will find that you are creating this link to pure consciousness yourself. It is not dependent on forcing yourself into a particular state of mind nor on believing in something outside yourself. It is experiential. It is effective, and it works.

Unless we have chosen the life of the monk, or the recluse withdrawn into his cave, we live life in the relative. It is the life of activity and the world, a world bombarded by stresses—the yelling, the bills, the daily disappointments. We may seek release in the thrill of mind-jolting music. We can live for a moment in the mental unity forced there by the racket. This is similar to when we sneeze or experience an explosion, and we are jolted into the moment. We may seek the violence and mayhem of the movies, the imagined love—the actors creating their fantasy characters for us to enjoy and escape into. But as we watch the image on the screen, we are there in the screen, not here within ourselves. It is a relief, perhaps. It is fun. It is an escape from the mental tennis match we play daily, hourly, moment by moment, with the children, our spouse, our boss, our colleagues, our friends—back and forth, back and forth—but movies and music are an escape from one reality into another. At our depths, do we seek a virtual life, or a virtuous life? Do we seek a life based in fantasy or a life based in reality?

I have found Transcendental Meditation—transcending—takes me in the direction of reality. Not outward into the sound and senses of the excitement of music and movies, but inward to a place of peace, a place of quiet that is my own, not manufactured and changing in the flickering light of the cinema, not in the beat and lyrics of the catchy song. A place instead where I am where I am when I am there, doing what I am doing in silence, and releasing the accumulated stresses of the daily world.

The technique allows those who practice it to experience finer and finer levels of the thinking process; our mind and body settle down, and the stresses in our system dissolve. Our metabolism slows; it is measurable. Our blood pressure lowers; it is measurable. We are there.

Gradually, over time, we transcend even the finest level of the thinking process and experience Transcendental Consciousness. We are aware only of being—only being in Being—our self in the Self—peaceful, whole, and complete. Our teacher will describe it like this: Just as the dye in the cloth takes hold and becomes more color-fast with each dipping into the vat and each fading in the sunlight, so do we become more complete, more aware, more secure in our self as we continue to practice Transcendental Meditation daily. And when we are in activity, we can be there— creating the character, designing the bridge, putting our child in the stroller, interacting with our audience, our child, our spouse, our friend with a sense of peace, wholeness, completeness, better able to deflect the negative remark, the overwhelming deadline, or this week's financial catastrophe.

The reality we experience practicing Transcendental Meditation is not a world of fantasy; it is not a world of battling evil. It is instead a world of strength, of peace and clarity, and it is accessible to each of us.

Transcendental Meditation will provide the experience of being there when you are there, and doing what you are doing when you are doing it, not only in the meditation; more importantly and over time, this experience will become infused into the reality of the world that faces you when you emerge from your twenty minutes of peace and solitude. You will find yourself stronger, more creative, and able to lead a more effective life.

The life of a monk is indeed hard. But one can bypass the struggle with the three evils. If we have chosen the life of the householder, with the practice of Transcendental Meditation it is possible to reach the Absolute, which the monk is seeking.

We don't have to renounce this life of activity, this life in the material world, which we enjoy so much. It is indeed possible *to bring the perishable aspect of life into living harmony with the imperishable.*

NINE

AUTHENTICITY

....

Being is the essential constituent of the individual...
Being is omnipresent in creation. It is the ultimate source of
all energy, intelligence, creativity, and activity.

MAHARISHI,
SCIENCE OF BEING AND ART OF LIVING

When I first learned Transcendental Meditation, I feared that it might be too great an adjustment to give up twenty minutes twice a day to "do nothing." How could I justify it? My time was too precious. My self-confidence rested on always being active and in control. Give up and turn inward? With reluctance.

After transcending with my first meditation, I was hooked. After a week, my productivity in the times I was not meditating soared. I could still be confident. I could still be productive, only now I could step back from my activity, almost be separate from it, and watch myself in action.

• • •

What is this new technique that is so old? How does it work? How do we know we can trust it?

Stop for a moment. Give yourself a long line. Allow yourself to explore for a while. Where would you go if you could go anywhere? Would you go to a place? To a person? Or nowhere—just remain where you are? You are giving yourself permission to do whatever you want—no job, no commitments, no one tugging at you for attention. What would you do? Would you sleep, or rest, read a book, take a walk, go shopping, or perhaps go find the people you love and be with them?

Just to think of it gives us pause. We have our plans, our obligations. We must do this, we must do that. How can we simply let go? But we're exploring here. For a moment, we are free of all the stuff of our life. We have given ourself permission. We can do whatever we want to do.

We might sink into a directionless state for a moment. We have to figure this thing out. This is an impossible place to be. We can't give up everything, even for a moment. We can't just drop out. Maybe we could go to sleep. God knows we need the rest, but we are too busy. Life has too many responsibilities. It sounds like fun perhaps, but it is not for us. It is not for you.

Reel yourself in for a moment...Slow down and stop...Take a pause...Listen to what is around you. Is it noisy? Is it silent? Are there any monkeys there clamoring for your attention?

Of course there are. We cannot stop thinking, not for a moment. It is our nature. We must do it. We must keep thinking thoughts, or we are nobody. We are lost without our thoughts. Thoughts give us our ideas and plans. Our plans lead us into action. Our actions make us feel good—or bad. Some actions do make us feel bad; we have to admit that. But if we weren't constantly active, what would we be? Who would we be? We need the TV. We need the budgets. We need the car. We need the place to live, the food to eat, the people around us. We need our activity. We need it all. It is who we are...Or is it?

Get up. Move to a quiet place, as quiet as you can find in your active life. It may be in an airport. It may be on the train or on a bus. It may be in a car with someone else driving, or it may be in the woods alone. It may be in a church by yourself in a pew. It may be in your own room. Wherever it is, look around. Sit down. Take a few breaths. You can think here, in silence. You can think here, even in the clamor of the airport gate. Sit down. Relax—wherever it is you find yourself, just sit quietly for a moment. You are here. You are quiet. It may be noisy around you, but inside you are quiet. Experience it. Listen to it...Where are you? Who are you? What is going on in that quietness where you find yourself?

Invariably there are thoughts. Focus on the wall for a moment. Focus on the airport crowd. Focus on the trees, the color of the room. There are still thoughts. There will always be thoughts. We can pray. There are still thoughts. As long as we try to get rid of the thoughts, they will return. They will always be with us. Focusing on something else doesn't seem to be the answer.

Let's say that for a moment we accept our thoughts. We recognize they are a natural part of who we are. They are essential to existence. How then do we still our mind? The more we think about stilling our mind, the harder it gets. We can't force it to be still. Our mind is not a three-year-old we can browbeat into submission with a time-out. But we want the rest, the relaxation that comes from stilling our mind. After all, that is what happens when we go to sleep. We tune out for a while, and we wake up refreshed—at least most of the time. We would like to have that refreshed experience perhaps and yet not get lost in sleep. We've been told, we sense, that there is more.

When you practice the Transcendental Meditation technique and settle down to finer levels of the thinking process, you will find that you have gone deeply into yourself. Inside, you have found a space—a space that is quiet and peaceful, a space without boundaries, a space that is yours and yours alone. You find that this is a space you can return to whenever you practice Transcendental Meditation. You have *transcended* the surface of life, the *relative* part of your existence. You have transcended the thoughts, you are at the source of thought, the *absolute* part of your existence. This space is unbounded. It is always there, and it goes on forever. This space is *pure consciousness.*

With Transcendental Meditation we have a technique to experience the Absolute. It is not dependent on belief: It is an experience, and we quickly realize that it is from here that we gain total relaxation, both mental and physical. It is from here that we gain immense strength. It is from this inner space of pure consciousness that we gain clarity of thought and peace of mind. It is from here that our actions truly emanate, and it is pure consciousness that is our ultimate source of joy and unbounded happiness. As Maharishi says, we have transcended to *the home of all the laws of Nature*—we have found our Self.

It is at this level of pure consciousness that the mind contacts universal Being, and it is in *Being* that you will reconcile the world of activity you live in daily with the world within you. It is a state of complete rest, and as Maharishi states: "Being is the essential constituent of the individual...Being is omnipresent in creation. It is the ultimate source of all energy, intelligence, creativity, and activity."

It is *Being* that joins us with ourselves, our work, our loves, our family, our children, our country, our religion, our values. It is *Being* that joins us with the world. It is in experiencing *Being* that the double binds are reconciled, and we realize our dharma, our duty in the world. Performing our dharma is not a chore. It causes us no irresolvable dilemmas, no loss of energy to do our duty, even when it may seem to conflict directly with other wants. We cannot be in London and Stockholm at the same time, but we do know absolutely where our duty lies, and we go to the place where we need to do it. We do the work that needs to be done, and we feel no regret for having had to make the choice.

The technique of Transcendental Meditation gives the concrete experience of the validity of inner life—inner pure consciousness at the source of thought. We experience this peaceful place during our meditation, and then we come out of our meditation and go about our business. We do not try to meditate while we are performing our daily activity. This would only divide our attention and make our activity less focused and less effective. Our lives as householders are fulfilled by focusing on and performing the actions of every moment of our lives to the best of our ability. This is the authentic life. This is the integrated life. This is the life of action, the life of Karma Yoga.

Our work, our life in the relative phase of existence, becomes the means to our growth—our growth to full enlightenment—our means to realizing our full potential. We become all we can be, for we are balancing the active part of our life with the peace, rejuvenation, and experience of pure Being in our twice-a-day practice of Transcendental Meditation.

For the recluse, it is the same. A recluse meditates and then performs his action, the action of contemplation and thought—not Karma Yoga, the path of action, but Gyana Yoga, the path of knowledge. Both paths, that of the householder and that of the recluse, are fulfilled by daily contact with this silence of Absolute Being, followed by their chosen activity.

It does not demand fervor. It does not demand that we have a religious conversion. We are not guilty; we are not sinners in this space. In this place of pure consciousness, each of us exists unblemished. We do not require forgiveness. There is no effort required to get there. And the experience is absolutely reproducible every day, twice a day, by simply closing our eyes and following the instructions we have been given for the Transcendental Meditation technique.

This technique is extraordinarily powerful. It is extraordinarily subtle. It is so subtle that at first you may not realize anything is happening, but this is why you have a TM teacher to show you the way to do it for the first few meditation sessions, and to be available thereafter to check your progress as often as needed.

Transcendental Meditation is unique. The monks of Mount Athos struggle with their perceived evils. Those on other paths struggle with theirs. Many say it requires years to achieve perfection. Perhaps it does, but with Transcendental Meditation, one simply practices the technique and then lives a normal life in activity, not worried about perfection. The activity we perform after meditation spontaneously becomes more effective, more life-supporting and beneficial to ourselves and those around us. We do not have to worry about being "spiritual" while we live life in activity. We do not have to apply ourselves to reading texts and performing rituals. We need simply to meditate and then go about our business. No rituals, no dogma, nothing but contact with pure consciousness, the source of thought that we experience through twice-daily meditation. We meditate, and then we "take it as it comes."

The authenticity that we experience and discover, the

integration that we feel in the meditation and the fullness we feel at our center gradually carry over to our life on the surface. In other words, we become our Self. We still have the daily barrage of thoughts, but we are no longer overwhelmed by them. We become more peaceful. We drop the airs, the inauthenticity that may have caused us to live the easily recognizable life of pretense and insecurity.

As for trusting that it is real? As with most things in our lives, we try them out. If over time we find that they work for us, we tend to stick with them. If they fail to work, or smack of falsehood, we drop them. Experience is the greatest teacher. Practice Transcendental Meditation, and you will quickly have the experience that it is real and that indeed "Being is the essential constituent of the individual...Being is omnipresent in creation. It is the ultimate source of all energy, intelligence, creativity, and activity."

TEN

LIVE YOUR DREAMS

....

*Maintaining your consciousness in the Self means maintaining
Self-consciousness while performing action...
This is brought about by regularly interrupting the
constant activity of the waking state of consciousness with
periods of silence in transcendental consciousness.*

MAHARISHI,
BHAGAVAD-GITA: A NEW TRANSLATION AND COMMENTARY
(Chapter III, Verse 30)

We make a choice when we let ourselves be overcome by the stresses that surround us. We can as easily make a choice to rise above them. We can deal with them. We can meditate. And as skeptical as I was before learning to meditate with TM, it took only a short time meditating for me to experience that meditation truly is a means to release our inner stresses and start with a clean slate. With a clean slate we can dream any dream unhindered by past restrictions and doubt. We can dream it, and we can achieve it.

• • •

All of us start from where we are. Successful or unsuccessful, happy or unhappy, driven or depressed—we start from where we are.

Imagine you are walking in the woods. Every tree has life. It seems every tree grows into its proper form. But on closer look, we see some that are misshapen for lack of light. Some are old and bent, broken from the storms that swept through. Some are less than they could be, for the soil around them is rocky and poor in nutrients. But those trees with the proper light, the deep soil, and room to grow—those trees are unstressed and grow to their proper form.

Come to the country. The fields have been plowed. The crops have been planted and have grown to full height. They sway in the wind; each stalk and fruit has achieved its perfect shape. Upon closer examination, however, some appear to be worm-eaten, or where a section of the field was flooded, the crop grew only to half its height—it is yellowed and withered. For some, too much sun has left them shriveled and dying. But those crops with the proper amount of light, the moist deep soil, and room to grow— those crops are unstressed and grow to their proper form.

Come to the city. People rush by on the sidewalk. Cars rush by on the street. The store windows draw us to their bright lights, and fashion displays lure us in. We stand and watch the people. We listen to the sounds. We live here. We love it here. We have enough money to enjoy what the city offers. We have the contacts and friends, we have the theaters and the restaurants, our apartment is just what we need, and we will meet our love later tonight for dinner. We turn the corner and see the beggar sitting there on the sidewalk, propped up against the building, his cup and sign held out for us to see—"Homeless...God bless you." We pause, drop in some coins, and continue on in the rush, and we wonder as we move on, How did the beggar get to where he is? And then we think, How did we get to where we are? What stresses befell the beggar that did not touch my life?

The woods, the country, the city—there are stresses everywhere. How can life be bliss? Is not life suffering, and is not deformity a part of life? It depends. For our own life, it depends on the cards we've been dealt, but it also depends on where we put our attention. We could just as well have been the beggar as who we are. We perhaps had that thought, and it scares us a bit. But most likely we had opportunities, an education, caring parents. We are seekers; we are survivors. We have learned to cope with whatever we had to do to get where we are.

We have stresses in life, but they have not overcome us. Neither could we say that life is perfect, of course. We don't always get everything we want. We fail now and then. But in general, we could say we have grown to our own "perfect form," for that is where we have put our attention—on success, on goals, on doing what we feel we need to do in life. There is suffering around us, and we view it with compassion. We see the broken trees, the failed crop. We help the beggar on the street, but for ourselves, we choose to focus on growth, on happiness, on the dreams of the brighter side of life.

Stress is the killer. Stress causes the deformed tree, the failed crop, the extreme of the beggar on the street. Stress touches each of us daily. Stress interferes with our getting what we want. Too much stress and we cannot think clearly. Too much stress and we cannot cope. Too much stress and we fail. Too much stress and our lives blow apart; our families blow apart. Too much stress and our countries go to war.

Transcendental Meditation relieves stress. Meditating twice daily takes us into a peaceful space that spontaneously and without effort dissolves whatever stresses are affecting us. We meditate and then come out gently to our activity, cleared out and free to function at our best. Whether we are the beggar, the president, or somewhere in between, we will find TM to be a reliable technique that will do this for us.

We live with desires and dreams of what we want, what is possible for us. We are motivated by our desires to achieve something. Where do desires come from? A desire is a thought. When we learn Transcendental Meditation, we experience that desires come pouring forth from a place deep within—from a place we experience as "the source of thought," and we become aware that the source of thought is a field of pure consciousness, which we reach when we transcend in meditation.

It is impossible to transcend when we are focusing on something or contemplating thoughts or daydreams, for that keeps our attention on the surface of the mind. Our brain and body stay stimulated. When we practice the Transcendental Meditation technique properly, we sink deep into a restful state, a physiologically measurable state that is deeper than the deepest sleep. As we reach the Transcendent, it is here that our mind contacts the source of thought—not intellectually, but experientially. It is here that we get the deep rest we need to come out and make the plans that will lead to the actions that will lead to the fulfillment of our desires. And it is the fulfillment of our desires on all levels that leads us to a life of happiness and bliss.

There are three states of consciousness with which we are

familiar—waking, dreaming, and sleeping. We know them. We experience them daily. Yet there is also a fourth state of consciousness, and when we practice Transcendental Meditation, this fourth state can become as common for us as waking, dreaming, and sleeping. It has been measured by scientists and compared physiologically to the three familiar states. It is a state of lowered blood pressure, increased brain wave coherence, lower blood lactate—an indicator of stress in the system—and numerous other significant physiological characteristics (see Appendix A). We access this fourth state of consciousness when we transcend during our practice of Transcendental Meditation. It is called *Transcendental Consciousness.*

We do not reach it when we stay focused on the surface of the mind. We do not reach it when we sit and contemplate. We do not reach it when we focus on the evils in our life, or the things we should not be doing, or our fears. When we focus on these things, our brain waves do not achieve coherence; our metabolism does not slow down as it does in the practice of Transcendental Meditation. We remain hovering on the surface, gripped by whatever our intellect tells us that we must avoid or achieve, focusing on whatever directives we have been taught to live by, whatever it is that the monkeys chatter, grin, and throw our way. It is simply a physiologically measurable fact. We do not transcend while we focus our mind on our thoughts.

Stress is the killer, and transcendence is the cure. How does Transcendental Meditation bring us to transcendence and this fourth state of consciousness? When we sleep well, we rebuild our body, we rest our mind, and we emerge refreshed. When we sleep poorly, we still obtain some level of rest, but if we are worried about the next meal, the loss of love, the bills waiting to be paid, or our poor performance, we toss and turn and awake sweating and miserable. We are not quite ready for the next day, and when we do have to face it, we do so grudgingly. We are not at our best. If only we had gotten the rest we need; if only we had slept well.

We are not avoiding life when we practice Transcendental Meditation. We are not being irresponsible by letting go of all the things bothering us at the moment. We are not being greedy or selfish, and we are not kidding our self. We have given our self permission to meditate, and the instructions given for meditation ensure that we will come out rested and renewed, ready for even more effective action.

We give our self permission to meditate, much in the way we give our self permission that it is time for bed. We consciously set aside the time and the space to turn inward. All the cares and rules, all of our thoughts and admonitions, are left on the surface. We bypass them in a manner similar to the way in which we fall asleep. We are never conscious of the moment when we pass from the waking state to the sleeping state and on to the dream state. Our body is just designed for it to happen. So it is with this form of meditation. It is a simple, natural, innocent process. In a manner similar to that in which we fall asleep and experience sleep, we begin the practice of Transcendental Meditation and "fall" into transcendence.

But in the state of Transcendental Consciousness, we do not sleep. This is a different state of mind and body. We may fall asleep during meditation if we are overly tired, but the state of transcendence itself is not sleep. In transcendence we experience that we are wide-awake. We are existing in a state that is similar to sleep in that we are totally resting, yet we are wide-awake inside. We are resting in a way that is unlike sleep, for we know we are wide-awake. We are awake, and we are experiencing a new and different form of consciousness. We have transcended, or gone beyond, the thinking process.

We go deep into a restful state in which we remain aware that we exist, yet this experience of pure existence is external to thoughts. The scientists who identified Transcendental Consciousness as a distinct fourth major state of consciousness called it a state of *restful alertness*. It is a state of expanded awareness, for there are no cares, no thoughts or troubles here. We exist in *Being*. It is consciousness in its purest form. It is the source of thought.

We are not kidding ourselves. We know we are awake, yet we know—we experience—that we are existing in our pure essence. Stresses simply disappear, similar to the way knots in our muscles are released when we get a massage. The knots in our mind and spirit are released with this form of meditation, which provides a technique for experiencing what exists in the restful alertness at the depths of our physiology, our mind, and our soul.

We have not chanted ourselves into exhaustion. We have not assumed a mood of piety and goodness. We have not battled with our self, the world, or the devil. All of that is irrelevant. We have taken a fork in the road pointed out to us by a wise man, a teacher who has guided us in a direction that has led to an inner source of sunlight and bliss, to pure rest and clarity of mind and spirit. We may be guilty on the surface, but here one feels in tune with one's Self and with the universe. We may feel broken and downtrodden in our daily life, but here we find a few moments of peace, relaxation, and clarity. From here the most evolutionary and life-supporting ideas pour forth. Here the dreams are made real. Here piety and goodness flow from us naturally and spontaneously. Here the solutions to our problems become self-evident. Here the deals are made on a win-win basis for the good of all concerned. Here the room is clean. Here life is orderly. Here we smile. Here we are our self. Here we bask in bliss.

If we choose to surrender ourselves to a "Higher Power," we choose to do so out of love and gratitude, not from fear or guilt, not from our sins and shortcomings. We have not had to exert tremendous effort, nor control our mind, nor force ourselves into an ethereal state of mind. We have simply followed a meditation technique given to us by a master who has the wisdom of the Vedic tradition, the most ancient wisdom cognized by the seers of India millennia ago. It is a system of total knowledge for living a productive, effective, and happy life. As Maharishi has stated, we are meant to be happy, and it is the stresses in our life that prevent happiness. Transcendental Meditation releases us from those stresses.

After twenty minutes of practicing our TM, we return to activity. We come out of meditation, just as we come out of a deep sleep, refreshed and ready for action. If we had not taken this fork in the road, consider where we might still be—battling with the cares of our life, the rules, the failures, the stresses. We would still be trying to deal with everything that exists down that other road without having had the benefit of this short break for rest and revitalization.

It is not that the problems and shortcomings have gone away. They are still there, just as they are still there when we awaken each morning. Only now we have experienced deep rest, and we are ready to handle them. We can practice the prayer and worship of our religion. We can make the business deal. We can go about our job. We can paint the picture, write the poem, care for our children, love our spouse. We can live our dreams, all with a clear head, with the renewed energy and vitality that we have gained by going deep within our self through this incredibly effective practice of Transcendental Meditation.

ELEVEN

WHOLENESS—COMPLETENESS

....

He whose self is established in Yoga,
whose vision everywhere is even, sees the Self in all beings,
and all beings in the Self.

MAHARISHI,
BHAGAVAD-GITA: A NEW TRANSLATION AND COMMENTARY
(Chapter 6, Verse 29)

I was a very good Methodist in my youth, president of my Methodist Youth Fellowship, a leader, a young preacher. It was totally fulfilling. At age nineteen, I traveled as an International Christian Youth Exchange student to Sweden and lived with a Swedish family for a year. It spelled the end of my adolescent certainty. The world was pretty broad, and I knew so little of it. College threw me for another loop. My conversion experiences counted for little amidst the incredible diversity of my friends and college courses. Life was a lot of work. I could no longer fall back on the experiences of my early teenage years and my religion for a sense of certainty; it took me until I was thirty to reorient and accept the fact that I was totally responsible for myself, sink or swim. No lover, no savior, no benign God on high was going to take care of me. Welcome to adulthood. It was up to me. Learning TM nearly forty years ago changed my life.

• • •

For those of us who have experienced a religious conversion, we know the feeling of an unshakable sense of wholeness. We have felt the presence of God in our lives, we have felt complete. It is not dissimilar to the feeling we experience when we fall in love. We feel whole; we feel complete. And it is not dissimilar to the feeling we have after performing a great feat and receiving the accompanying recognition—again, we feel whole, we feel renewed, we feel complete. These are life's peak experiences. Our sense of who we are is subsumed into something—or someone—greater than our self, and we expand in heart, mind, and body. We walk taller than before. We speak stronger than before. We smile and thank our lucky stars that we have been shined on. We bask in the glory. We bask in the love and well-being we feel from

God, from our love, from those around us who are recognizing us for our true worth.

And it is real. When it happens to us, this feeling is probably one of the most real things in our life. If we have been fortunate enough to have experienced the presence of God, the warmth and presence of a true love, or the recognition and acclaim for a job well done, there is little more that we need in life. We have achieved happiness. However we got here, we are the flower that has unfolded in the sunlight; we are chosen; we have arrived. We have arrived, and we want to stay here. We desperately want to stay here in this place, this state of mind of wholeness and completeness. Just a little while longer—like forever. We want to stay here, but we know that it is not possible. The applause must stop. We must rise up from our knees, arise from the bed; our children must grow up and leave us; our jobs will not be there forever. We ourselves will grow old and die. Yet still we struggle. We want to maintain, rediscover, this feeling of completeness, this sense of wholeness, of happiness in our life.

We can get so caught up in achievement and accomplishments, attempting to support this person who is our self, that we often forget the sources of our completeness. We get too busy to go to our religious service, too busy to spend time with our love, too busy to stop and realize that the sense of completeness has gone—evaporated, passed from our consciousness. We then experience the resulting suffering and disappointments. We are alone again—reliant on our insufficient self. We backslide. We go to prayer meetings. We look again for a renewal of love. We scheme and plan for the next big breakthrough, our next accomplishment that will bring us the acclaim we seek. We continually look outside of our self for our salvation and sense of completeness—our sense of wholeness and happiness.

When we were complete and whole, our health blossomed, our worries receded, we felt confident in our ability to converse and move beyond who we were. We had the spirit in us. We were masters of our fate. We felt we existed in God's hand, and so we did.

People begin meditation for many reasons. You have heard perhaps that it holds out the promise of enlightenment. What is that? Is that the perpetual high we experienced from God's presence, or love, or accomplishment? No, it is not. If we want the flashy experience of a conversion, or a first love, or a peak accomplishment, we have to accept the fact that the high will not stay with us without changing. We simply cannot live a perpetual high. We will eventually break down. We cannot live a perpetual sense of conversion. We cannot live a perpetual anything. Life is change. Perhaps that is what we realize when we meditate. Perhaps that is why wise men say it takes a lifetime to achieve perfection, a lifetime to become enlightened, a lifetime to become at one and at peace with the entire universe. Life is never perpetual perfection, as we have sometimes all too painfully learned. Life is perpetual process.

And yet we can, we must, live the process. We must get up every morning, feed the dog, feed the child, feed ourselves. We must dress and go to work. We can, indeed we must, live the process necessary for maintaining our life and supporting the lives of those around us, those depending on us. How well we do that, and in what state of mind we do that, will determine our sense of perfection, our sense of wholeness and completeness—our sense of happiness. How well we do that may give us a glimpse of the state of unity of body and mind and perpetual contentment.

On the other hand, life in the fast lane can be exciting, but it can also be short and disappointing. It can be dangerous, and we can easily lose our way. It may, however, be irresistible. At some point in our life—perhaps even daily—we yearn to experience this sense of wholeness, this sense of the sparks flying, this sense of accomplishment, this sense of a greater presence, the kiss of a loved one, the shake of a hand, the recognition from another that we exist.

All of us yearn for positive experiences, and we strive and

struggle to make them happen. Some of us strive and struggle with drugs and intimacy, some with sports and work, some with banter or prayer. Some convert, some move on, some seek, and some find. We find whatever we can to bolster ourselves and reaffirm that we are strong, vital, productive, creative, and happy. We do whatever we need to do to create ourselves—our sense of self—and the more exciting the better. The joy of new discovery is irresistible. If it is around the next corner, we want it. If we don't get it, we can become miserable. If we don't get it for long enough, we can become depressed and give up, or, if we can summon the strength, we can become circumspect and try to figure out the problem. What will it take to restore ourselves to the self we know we want?

Creating a sense of self requires constant nourishment. In a sense, we write a check daily, hourly, moment by moment, drawing on our personal account of who we are. We make deposits into that account as often as we can—a new friend, a new car, a new love, a better story, and sometimes, perhaps even a lie. If we can't write a legitimate check on our account, some of us will fall back and live on our credit—someday I'll do this, someday I'll do that, someday I'll pay you, but for now I am flashy, and I am OK: I'm watching TV, and I'm feeling good.

Deep down, below the surface, we know vaguely who we are. Deep in ourselves we know how much we really have in our account. With some reflection, we will know if we are just soaking it up from the TV, or if it is really there in our accomplishments, our true love, our actions and interactions with others. Deep down, if we take the time to look, to live in the moment, we have a sense of self—of who we are.

People begin meditation for many reasons. The flashy comes, and it is gone. The recognition, the conversion, the intimacy, all were wonderful, but one cannot live them perpetually. One must recreate them continually. It is simply a fact of life that we must get used to—constant nourishment, continual deposits into our personal account, and if necessary credit, are all required for survival, but what to do when our account is depleted and our credit runs out? Work harder of course, and we may be very successful replenishing things for ourselves, but if we're not careful, it may also be too late.

Through meditation it is possible to experience a sense of Self—our small self as part of a greater Self. Our self experiences Self. The child foresees the man. The child foreshadows the woman. The perfect form of the tree, the plant, the flower, the person, exists in a state of pure consciousness; the pure form—our pure form—exists in the unstressed state of Transcendental Consciousness which we experience when we learn Transcendental Meditation, the state in which we recognize that we ourselves are part of a greater Self. At the source of thought in pure consciousness, one experiences the greater Self. And the greater Self is common to everything. It is the Unified Field, from which everything in existence comes forth, that is experienced with Transcendental Meditation.

It is from this recognition and experience of the Self that we gain our experience of wholeness and completeness, independent of possessions, independent of recognition, independent of the ups and downs of daily living. The changes we cannot avoid, the peaks and valleys, the good, the bad, the love-me-love-me-not equations of daily life—all level out in the Self, the experience of Yoga (Unity) that exists beneath the surface of daily life and activity, and it is accessible to everyone through this *safe* and *reliable* practice of Transcendental Meditation.

If somebody handed you a ticket to the Mets game or the opera or the ballet—a free ticket— you'd probably take it. If someone told you of a Macy's sale—suddenly they were giving away two for one—you'd rush right down. If someone gave you a tip on the hottest stock with a guarantee to double your money in a week, would you buy it? Or the keys to a new car, or an introduction to someone who would be a perfect match for you, or access to a new school or program or teacher that would guarantee success for your child, or the most peaceful, pleasant vacation you could imagine for yourself and a loved one—would you get on board? Would you check it out?

You can imagine all these things—you can perhaps see them in your mind's eye—the game, the show, the new clothes, the money, the car, the perfect match for you, the happy kid, the relaxation for you and a love. They suddenly become as good as real in your mind, and you would probably take whatever action you have to take to have them—reach out and take the ticket, purchase the stock, take the keys, ask for the date, interview the teacher, make reservations for the vacation.

It is our nature to want more and more. It is our nature to gravitate toward what will make us happy, and we will take whatever action is necessary to turn perceived objects of happiness from simply daydreams and fantasy into reality.

There is a difference between the intellectual study of something and actually doing it in practice—tennis, for instance. We can read all we want about tennis, but until we put on our tennis shoes, pick up the racquet, and walk out on the court, it's all a dream. Like little children, we can imagine the greatest fantasy of success and accomplishment, until we pick up the racquet and hit our first ball. Life isn't lived in the abstract. We don't fall in love in the abstract. We fall in love with the body and breath of a living human being two inches from our lips.

Our golf game languishes until we practice. The golf magazine is a help, but we have to go out and play. The solution to the math problem can be imagined in the abstract, but until we set to work and solve the equations, it remains in the abstract. The business deal can be imagined in the abstract, but until we call the bank, carry through on the negotiations, reach agreement, and sign the papers, it remains in the abstract. No money changes hands.

It may be useful to imagine our tennis game, our golf game,

our love, our equations, and the business deal in the abstract. It may be useful to think about them, but only as the precursor to the actual performance. We can rehearse in our mind the perfect swing of the racquet or the club, the perfect words leading to consummation of the kiss, the process of solving the equations, the negotiation process and reaching agreement on the business deal—having the perfect form and the steps to perfection in mind when we begin the actual process of the activity will assist us and guide us to the best possible performance, whatever it is we seek to do.

Imagine, however, that as we start the activities we have imagined, studied, and planned for, we are hampered by a headache, worried sick about how we will perform, feeling guilty about our lack of performance the last time we tried this activity. Imagine we are convinced that we are simply meant to suffer in life, that we have no right to success in what we are setting out to do. Imagine that we have been told by our boss, our lover, our colleague, that we are an idiot with no skill whatsoever. We were creamed last time in the tennis game; we came in last in our foursome at golf; instead of kissing us, our lover walked away in anger; we failed to solve the equation the last ten tries; and we lost a small fortune when we inaccurately analyzed the outcome of our last stock purchase or business deal. How is our performance then?

If we allow our self to be defined by people and forces external to our self, we will be forever at their mercy. If we set out to perform an activity slowed by fatigue, or depression, or a negative image of who we are and what we want to achieve, we are less likely to get the results we desire. Our physical and mental state of mind have a great deal to do with how well we perform.

We can take steps to prepare ourselves for peak performance externally by limiting whom and what we let into our life. Do we heed every negative comment, every criticism, or do we surround ourselves with positive support from friends, coaches, and teachers whenever possible? Our choice will make a difference. We can prepare ourselves internally for peak performance by getting adequate rest, eating proper foods, and filling our mind with positive, uplifting thoughts, images, and ideas, versus the sensationalism and mayhem that fill our mind when we expose our self to the TV eight to ten hours a day.

Outside direction and criticism can have their place. They can be useful to constructive shaping and improvement of our activity when balanced with positive encouragement. Self-examination also has its place, but we need to be careful about becoming overwhelmed by our own negativity, fatigue, and loneliness.

A sense of wholeness and completeness can be achieved, in part from the successful accumulation of possessions, in part from the successful outcome of activity, in part from a loving, supportive environment we create by our selection of friends, our mental images of who we are and how we fit into the cosmos. We can take an active role in creating who we are by whom and what we choose to allow into our life. But if we fail to choose, we can find that *no* choice often becomes *the* choice. We can move sloppily through activity and relationships allowing chance alone to shape our fate, or we can take an active role in the decisions and directions that will bring us the most success and happiness.

It is possible to live the life of more-and-more. It is possible to bypass the experience that life is meant to be suffering. It is possible to make the leap from the intellectual understanding of what we have to do to be successful to the actual experience of being successful. We can take an active role in creating our way of life by choosing to learn Transcendental Meditation. The daily practice of TM provides a direct link to our unblemished, rested, positive self. We can read all we want to about it. But as with the golf and tennis games, it is the doing of it that produces positive results.

The practice of TM produces energy and a balanced frame of mind as a result of the deep rest you get when you meditate. It produces optimum activity when you come out to swing the club, discipline your kid, kiss your love, and make the choices that create your sense of self and place in the world—for you will have left behind the stresses, the worries, the hindrances to optimum performance, the hindrances to creating a sense of completeness, wholeness, and happiness in your life.

Learn the Transcendental Meditation technique and by practicing it for twenty minutes twice a day you will experience wholeness; you will experience completeness; you will become the person, as stated in the ancient Vedic text of the *Bhagavad-Gita,* "whose self is established in Yoga, whose vision everywhere is even, sees the Self in all beings, and all beings in the Self."

TWELVE

LIVING WITHOUT STRESS: "TAKE IT AS IT COMES"

....

Medical researchers have shown that a large proportion of physical disorders arise primarily from mental tension as a result of anxieties and failures in life.

MAHARISHI,
SCIENCE OF BEING AND ART OF LIVING

The existence of so much suffering in the world does not mean that suffering should be accepted as our normal state of existence. Think back to the tree in the woods, the crops in the field. Unstressed, the tree and the crops grow to their perfect form. Unstressed, we, too, grow to our perfect form. But life is full of stress.

• • •

Over the years, I have had a good-natured disagreement with a close friend. He happens to be a Buddhist. My friend says the Buddhists teach that the way to avoid suffering is to give up desires. For a while I had to agree, because giving up desires helped me through a rough period in my life. But after learning TM, I quickly stabilized emotionally, and then realized that there is more to life than avoiding suffering. I realized that for me *giving up* desires was not the path to accomplishment. It was not the path to happiness. The way to accomplishment and happiness was to *fulfill* my desires. No longer hobbled by a restriction on my desires, I was free to remarry, build a business, and become more successful and happier than I could ever have imagined.

It may help to give up desires temporarily in an attempt to stabilize our mind, but most of us are people of action—we live a life of action, of Karma Yoga. We want things. We want loving relationships. We want success. We live life in the world. Most of us have not withdrawn into the monastic life of the recluse. Most of us would rather suffer, if that is what it takes to have some success and possessions, than simply give up desires and lead the life suited to the recluse. On the other hand, this suffering is not fun.

The path of action is a recognized path to self-realization in the Vedic tradition: Successful action, right action without attachment to one's desires, and in balance with the deep rest one gains from the practice of TM, can bring one to a state of happiness and fulfillment, even to the place of enlightenment.

Maharishi brings us a solution to suffering based on the Vedic tradition: *"Perform action, but do not get attached to the fruits of action."* And the way to avoid attachment to the fruits of action is to take the mind back to the Self, the source of thought. That is the key to successful action without attachment to the results. It is the key to minimizing disappointment. It is the key to avoiding the suffering we experience when we are unsuccessful at getting what we want. Work, perform our duty—our dharma—to the best of our ability, and then let it go. Don't force it. Don't lament if it does not lead to immediate success. Act, but do not get attached to the results, to the "fruits of the action."

We can—we should—desire. It is right and proper to want more and more. It leads to our growth and development. Desires for more and more are part of our evolution. But avoid suffering by avoiding attachment to the outcomes of our actions. Practice Transcendental Meditation and we find that more and more comes our way spontaneously, without intense effort, without strain, without attachment, and without suffering. If a particular desire remains unfulfilled, we nonetheless have the calm and peace, the sense of certainty and confidence at our very center, which we experience from having meditated with this technique. Basically, we experience in transcendence that we are whole and complete, independent of the outcome of our actions. Suffering is not our normal state of existence, and we need not give up our desires to know this for ourselves.

Just as in practicing the Transcendental Meditation technique we don't struggle to have some flashy experience, so it is in activity. We take the benefit of the rest we have achieved in our meditation—the clear thought, the renewed energy, the experience of the Absolute—and we do our work. We do our work without struggling, but we also add a very simple thing—we take it as it comes. Maharishi has compared this to the Christian tenet: *Let*

Thy Will Be Done. This simple direction can make the difference between experiencing peace and equanimity or pain and suffering in our daily lives. We can pucker up, but it may not lead to the kiss. That's OK. Take it as it comes. We can ask for the raise, but we may not get it. That's OK. Take it as it comes. We can sit and watch TV, for we need a break for a while, and that's OK. Take it as it comes.

The result is a secret bypass around anxiety. This is not a mood; it is a frame of mind that is spontaneously cultivated through our regular practice of Transcendental Meditation, and it leaves us free to rethink our approach without a lot of baggage and worry about failure. We are not attached. By taking it as it comes, we keep ourselves free from the often debilitating frame of mind we incur from momentary failure. We remain clear and able to regroup and act effectively. We can act and just let things take their course, knowing that the results will correspond directly to the effectiveness of our actions.

When we transcend in meditation, we experience ourselves at our quietest, our purest, our most relaxed. Dye and sun. Dye and sun. Activity and rest. Activity and rest. That is what we are doing through the regular alternation of activity and meditation during the day. It is that which brings out the purity and clear thought we need to effectively perform action. And it is effective action that brings about the fulfillment of our desires.

Attachment to the results divides our thinking. We are so busy thinking about the good grade we need that we fail to solve the equation. Time is up, and we have to turn in the paper. We are so busy thinking about all the money we are going to make that we miss the deadline for submission of the purchase offer. Our mind is divided and our action is ineffective. By letting go, by meditating and taking it as it comes, our mind becomes free to focus in the moment on whatever activity it is we have chosen to perform. And we know that when we focus entirely on what it is that needs doing, we can do our best job. The results will follow spontaneously, based on the effectiveness of the action.

We do not meditate to escape from life. We meditate to become more effective in life. It is the deep rest we find in our twenty minutes of Transcendental Meditation twice a day that carries over into activity.

We do not accomplish anything in meditation. Accomplishments happen in activity. Meditation leaves the mind and body rested, ready to perform activity. Meditation produces the clear day regardless of what is confronting us, for we don't fight what comes our way. We take it as it comes. With the deep rest we experience in meditation, more often than not we find that when we come out of meditation to perform activity, our thoughts, skills, and reason are on notice, more keenly available for performing effective action, saying the proper thing that needs to be said, performing the right action for the moment, making the life-supporting decisions that need to be made—all of which well up from deep within us in an almost miraculous way, without pride, without self-congratulation. It all just happens naturally and spontaneously.

How on earth can you set aside twenty minutes twice a day for Transcendental Meditation? How can you stop everything twice a day and still get everything done? Think about your day. How much time do you spend vacillating in indecision? How much time do you spend in idle conversation, or watching the tube? If you were to do a time analysis of your day, how much wasted time is there in your schedule?

It doesn't matter really. For we find when we begin TM that we naturally become more efficient. More and more, we find that each day we are operating at our best. Our thoughts become clearer. Our decisions don't take nearly as long. Almost every day is a clear day. The time we spend meditating before breakfast and before dinner (those are the times recommended), are more than made up by our increased efficiency and effectiveness.

Are you already successful? Transcendental Meditation will only increase your success. Are you miserable? If the lack of fulfillment of your desires has really got you down, don't give up your desires. Instead, learn TM. Over time, TM will relieve your stress, neutralize your suffering, enable you to perform more successful action. It will gradually replace your suffering with fulfillment of desires, and you will experience the resulting happiness that brings. As Maharishi says, man's natural state without stress is happiness. The regular practice of Transcendental Meditation relieves stress and enables us to experience happiness.

Research has shown that Transcendental Consciousness is a measurable state physiologically: The left and right hemispheres of the brain experience synchrony of brain wave patterns during deep meditation (see Appendix A). We experience this sensation physically when we meditate with Transcendental Meditation.

Gradually, the state of transcendence can carry over into our waking life. Gradually, like dipping the cloth many times into the dye, we may become aware of continuing to experience Transcendental Consciousness while performing activity. If this does happen, we don't get attached to it. We continue to take it as it comes. But this fifth state of consciousness, in which the peace and awareness of transcending in meditation grow and begin to accompany us full time in our waking state, Maharishi calls Cosmic Consciousness. If we start to experience it, great; it is pleasant. If we are not yet experiencing it, great, for we already have a more effective, more productive, happier life than before learning Transcendental Meditation. We have a technique for managing the stresses in our lives and whatever happens, we just—*take it as it comes.*

THIRTEEN

WHY DOES IT WORK?

....

*When the conscious mind transcends and attains
the state of Being, it becomes one hundred percent
of the state of Being…(It) loses its individuality and becomes
cosmic mind…When the mind comes back into the field of
relative life, it gains individuality again, but it also seems to
retain some of the great unbounded, universal status which
it had just attained.*

MAHARISHI,
SCIENCE OF BEING AND ART OF LIVING

Several years ago, I spent two years developing and constructing a six-story luxury apartment building in our town. Throughout the year-long actual construction process, I held weekly job meetings with the architect, the contractor, and all the tradesmen to discuss our progress and identify problems before they arose. My electrical contractor was someone who had worked for me for fifteen or more years on various projects. During his vacations, he was a mountain climber and extremely fit at fifty-some years of age. He was not the job foreman, but each week at the job meeting I found myself impressed at the overview he had of the entire construction process. He was never afraid to point out potential coordination problems between the trades, whether they related directly to his electrical installations or not. One day after a job meeting, he stayed behind to speak with me. "I heard you do TM," he said to me. "That's true," I replied. "I've done it myself for thirty-five years," he told me. He is an extremely bright guy, but for me the fact that he practiced the TM technique explained his calm clarity of thought and his ability to see immediately to the heart of a problem. His disclosure simply reinforced my conviction that this meditation really does work. I found out later that his wife does it as well.

• • •

Transcending has been assumed to belong exclusively to the experience of saints or at least to the very religious. The active person living his or her daily life seldom has time for the deep transition into what the saints have struggled mightily to achieve—an expansion of self into an experience of God's presence—or what William Wordsworth or Ralph Waldo Emerson found in Nature: a heightened awareness of oneself and unity with all creation.

As householders, we are typically not saints and poets. We struggle with our bills, our children, and each other. That love we found requires constant renewal and is often overcome by routine. Only occasionally do we experience the bliss of each other's presence. Our walk in the woods, or by the water, a sunset or moonrise, remind us of our place in Nature for a few moments. Our prayers at church or temple or mosque get us through to the next week. But in between, life in the relative can be fraught with problems.

Maharishi's unique contribution was to bring his ancient tradition of meditation, founded in the knowledge of the Vedas, handed down through thousands of years from teacher to teacher, and to make it available to every one of us in our living room, our yurt, our palace, our cathedral. He deciphered the *Baghavad-Gita* for us in his *Translation and Commentary* and explained that ultimate spiritual development is not confined just to the saint, the *sanyasi* in the Himalayas, or the hermit in his cave on Mount Athos.

It is available to the people like my electrician who work for a living every day. It is available to the leaders of the world and to the prisoners in Folsom State Prison, where a study was done on the beneficial results experienced by prisoners who learned Transcendental Meditation. It is available to the army in Ecuador, where six hundred soldiers learned TM in March of 2010. It is available to the monks in Thailand, where a Japanese teacher of Transcendental Meditation recently instructed three thousand Buddhist monks. It is available to the schoolchild and the athlete, to the doctor at our hospital and the professor at our university. There is not a person in the world who cannot learn it and who will not benefit from having learned Transcendental Meditation.

As a trained teacher of Transcendental Meditation will tell you, "The only prerequisites to learning TM are that you have a human nervous system and that you be able to think a thought." It is that simple. It is a mechanical, reproducible process that opens us to a world within—the very world that has been opened to the saints. It may take years to achieve their level of ecstasy, or we may never achieve that, but our lives will improve the longer we do the technique. With our very first meditation we can transcend to a place of no thought, no action, no duties, no problems. It is a unique state of pure existence, pure Being—a state of awareness that ties us to all creation.

The priests, the pastors, the professors, the professionals who learn it report this experience. The students, the electricians, the laborers, the skeptics, once they have learned and followed the instructions, find this experience, and it grows. It may be faint at first. It may take a few meditations to realize that something unusual is going on, for it is delicate. It disappears if you exert effort to make it work, but when the process is followed with the proper instruction, everyone reports similar experiences. As the stresses in our system are released through the practice of TM, our experiences of Being only become deeper and purer.

Paul Gelderloos, a psychologist from the Netherlands, writes in his book *Valuation and Transcendental Meditation* that one TM course participant reported an experience during meditation to Maharishi:

"I was deep in pure consciousness beyond all thought and relative concerns, and often felt that I never wanted to come out of this supremely perfect peace. Meditation was filled with light and bliss. I experienced pure consciousness as an unbounded and synchronized continuum—and in this state I was all that is."

Gelderloos has done his own extensive research on Transcendental Meditation and on the experiences of saints and ascetics who reported remarkable experiences of Being. He goes on to say: "We find different expressions (of transcendental consciousness) but they all indicate a sameness of experience, which is expressed as a kind of 'no experience.' It is the state of complete fulfillment, which is almost impossible to describe in words."

This experience is not at all incompatible with our religion.

In fact, it is the experience we seek in our religion—the sense of unity, this sense of being present in all creation. TM simply provides a technique that assists us in getting there. It is what the mystics and the saints achieve with dedication and devotion. This is what we occasionally achieve in our prayers and religious rituals. But even the saints cannot maintain this feeling of God's presence continuously, nor even return to it necessarily at will, and its loss can often be devastating to their well-being—producing the spiritual crisis known as the "dark night of the soul."

As stress is released in Transcendental Meditation, we transcend into deep rest and sometimes to an experience of Being, and this experience of Being opens us to a sense of awe, much like an unbelievably beautiful sunset. What we do with it is ours to choose. Whatever it is, we return to our life on the surface, life in the relative. We continue to do our duty. We continue to practice our religious faith, but whatever we do, we have experienced the depths of life, the depths of our being. We are refreshed, and we can go back to this experience whenever we meditate—whenever we perform this technique we have been taught.

A sense of unity with all creation is something sought by the religious, and indeed is something promised in every religion, but even if it is found, the knowledge fades, the fervor dwindles. It can get lost in the very dogma and ritual that are supposed to help us produce this inner peace and sense of the Self, for dogma and ritual lie on the surface. They are some of the very distractions that keep our attention in the relative and prevent us from accessing the life within. Prayer can help, but it is often short and full of supplication, and it can also remain on the surface and in the relative—give me this, give me that, help me through this, help me through that. The connection to the unlimited source of power within us cannot be easily and readily accessed without a technique which bypasses the relative and allows access to this inner world of Being.

Practitioners of Transcendental Meditation do not have a

monopoly on achieving an experience of inner peace and bliss. This experience is a necessary part of the human condition as much as laughter, as much as love. In the right frame of mind, we may find it in the mountains. We may find it at the seashore. We may find it in the sunset when we stop all the chatter and take the time to experience this elemental phenomenon of Nature. We may experience it when we run a mile, or clean the garage to perfection, or make our bed precisely. We may experience it in the glow of deep conversation with a friend, or the perfect glass of wine. We may experience it when we solve a problem, write a poem, make a business deal, or tune an engine to perfection.

It is not a secret, this inner state of peace and well-being. We can experience it in the practice of our religion. We can experience it in love and the touch of a baby's skin—in the love and touch of each other. While inner peace and bliss may be found when we listen and pay attention, while they may be there when we create a sense of mindfulness, we often find that these experiences which produce inner peace and bliss can be fleeting and not easily repeatable, dependent more on chance, and they are not necessarily the deep experiences of Being.

What Maharishi has done is to re-enliven the knowledge of the Vedas, which set forth a technique for systematically accessing the state of Being. He teaches a simple technique that requires no change of lifestyle, no change of dress, no public proclamation that we do Transcendental Meditation. It is neither a directive toward salvation nor a threat of guilt and suffering if we don't perform it.

The Transcendental Meditation technique is compatible with the life of the businessman on the airplane, the teacher in the classroom, the pastor leading a congregation, the mechanic caring for the cars of his customers, the shopkeeper, the poet, the athlete who yearns for enhanced performance, the seeker who seeks in vain, the artist who suffers through each creation, the monk in his cell, the nun in her convent, the soldier, the politician, the worker in the mine, the young child confused by growing up. Anyone, everyone, can take advantage of the benefits offered by this simple technique of Transcendental Meditation.

By transcending into *Being* twice a day, we find we come forth stronger, more centered, and more able to focus on the work we have chosen to do.

As Maharishi states, "When the mind comes back into the field of relative life, it gains individuality again, but it also seems to retain some of the great unbounded, universal status which it had just attained..."

FOURTEEN

WHO DOES IT?

....

*Whatsoever a great man does, the very same is
also done by other men. Whatever the standard he sets,
the world follows it.*

MAHARISHI,
BHAGAVAD-GITA: A NEW TRANSLATION AND COMMENTARY
(Chapter 3, Verse 21)

All my life I have been fortunate to have had teachers, guides, and mentors, people who have shown me the way to perfect a task, stay out of trouble, improve my life—people I could look up to and whose advice I could choose to follow. Or not.

• • •

Award-winning film director, writer, and producer David Lynch has been practicing Transcendental Meditation for over thirty years. In his book *Catching the Big Fish* he tells us, "I have been 'diving within' through the Transcendental Meditation technique for over 30 years. It has changed my life, my world. I am not alone. Millions of other people of all ages, religions, and walks of life practice the technique and enjoy incredible benefits."

In July 2005, David Lynch established the David Lynch Foundation for Consciousness-Based Education and World Peace to help finance scholarships for students in middle and high schools to learn the Transcendental Meditation technique and to fund research on the technique and its effects on learning.

On April 4, 2009, at Radio City Music Hall in New York City, the David Lynch Foundation sponsored the "Change Begins Within" concert featuring a host of performers who practice Transcendental Meditation: Paul McCartney, Ringo Starr, Donovan, Sheryl Crow, Eddie Vedder, Moby, Bettye LaVette, Ben Harper, Jerry Seinfeld, Howard Stern, and Mike Love of the Beach Boys.

Paul McCartney of the Beatles spoke from stage, guitar in hand, and had this to say about TM: "It was a great gift Maharishi gave us. For me it came at a time when we were looking for something to stabilize us—it was the end of the sixties. It was a delightful gift that you can call on at any time." The Beatles had learned

TM and spent time with Maharishi in Rishikesh, India, in 1968.

David Lynch stated that since the launching of his foundation, he has supported over 150,000 inner-city students who have begun utilizing the TM technique "to eliminate traumatic stress that undermines academic achievement and short-circuits lives. These students have dramatically better test scores, grades, and graduation rates, while dropout rates, suspensions, and expulsions have greatly decreased. The program has the full-hearted support of superintendents, principals, faculty, students, and parents."

In December 2010, my wife and I received an invitation to attend his second annual "Change Begins Within Benefit Event." His invitation read as follows: "I am proud to invite you to the second 'Change Begins Within' benefit on Monday December 13, at The Metropolitan Museum of Art in New York City. Russell Brand, Clint Eastwood, Dr. Mehmet Oz, Katy Perry, Russell Simmons, myself, and other very special guests will be part of a very different and exciting evening..."

We attended and heard his introduction from the auditorium stage as he said, "More groups of people from all walks of life have come to embrace our program, including veterans suffering from post-traumatic stress disorder and their families; homeless adults; children from the streets of Harlem and East LA; American Indians subsisting on impoverished reservations; and incarcerated men and women locked away in maximum security penitentiaries. And the demand has never been greater in New York City, in particular among local schools, veterans groups, and homeless shelter re-entry programs."

The reach of David Lynch's foundation extends beyond students and the homeless to the Operation Warrior Wellness program, in which he is attempting to reach thousands of returning veterans of armed conflict with the benefits of learning Transcendental Meditation. At the December 13, 2010, benefit, half a dozen military officers and soldiers in uniform lined up on the stage before us to affirm their support for this program. Several spoke, both live and on a video screen that stretched across the stage, about their experiences in war and the post-traumatic stress disorder from which they had suffered. They had returned to their lives and families devoid of feelings and emotions, unable to express themselves to their loved ones and their friends. One veteran, speaking through tears, said of TM, "The first time I meditated, I experienced this sense of relief…," and a second veteran said simply: "My life came back."

"Children of the Night" is another program within David Lynch's Change Begins Within initiative, designed to teach TM to young women who spend their lives on the streets. One woman, discreetly backlit to protect her identity, spoke to the audience of seven hundred of us about how Transcendental Meditation had helped her to break the vicious cycle of living on the streets and all that entailed. Practicing TM restored her sense of dignity and enabled her to establish a productive, independent life of her own.

Film director Martin Scorsese, speaking to the audience via video, said, "For the last few years I've been practicing meditation. It's difficult to describe the effect it's had on my life. I can only mention maybe a few words: *calm*, *clarity*, a *balance*, and, at times, a *recognition*. It's made a difference. On this night, as you're trying to raise the funds necessary to bring Transcendental Meditation to students, veterans, homeless men and women, Native Americans, anyone suffering from strong stress, I want to thank you…"

Hollywood actor and director Clint Eastwood also spoke to us via video in the auditorium of the Metropolitan Museum of Art, reaffirming the benefits his forty-year practice of Transcendental Meditation has brought to his work and creativity. I had first heard him speak about his daily TM routine in the 1970s, when he appeared with Maharishi on *The Merv Griffin Show*.

David Lynch's website (www.davidlynchfoundation.org) provides a complete picture of the work the foundation is doing, as well as detailed interviews and performances from this benefit event. He writes about the purpose of his foundation: "Our Foundation was established to ensure that any child in America who wants to learn and practice the Transcendental Meditation program can do so. The TM program is the most thoroughly researched and widely practiced program in the world for developing the full creative potential of the brain and mind, improving health, reducing stress, and improving academic outcomes. We provide scholarships for students to learn the technique and to receive the complete follow-up program of instruction throughout their student years to ensure they receive the maximum benefits. We also provide scholarships for students who want to attend the growing number of highly successful schools, colleges, and universities founded on this Consciousness-Based approach to education...In today's world of fear and uncertainty, every child should have one class period a day to dive within himself and experience the field of silence—bliss—the enormous reservoir of energy and intelligence that is deep within all of us. This is the way to save the coming generation."

And speaking of the students he has met who are practicing this technique of "diving within," he said they are "all unique individuals, very much themselves. They are amazing, self-sufficient, wide-awake, energetic, blissful, creative, powerfully intelligent and peaceful human beings."

Meeting these students, he said, was proof that Consciousness-Based education is "a profoundly good thing for our schools and for our world." He credits Maharishi with "revolutionizing the lives of millions of people."

While each of us will realize for ourselves the personal validity of the practice of Transcendental Meditation, it is nonetheless interesting to hear of others—artists, celebrities, politicians, scientists, business wizards—people at the top of their game who find TM a wonderful support for their personal life, their success and happiness.

Comedian Jerry Seinfeld, in an interview in the *Philadelphia Inquirer*, spoke about the effect of Transcendental Meditation in his life: "I've been practicing Transcendental Meditation most of my life. I think that it does something to your nervous system...It has given me a calmness I don't think I had at nineteen."

Musician Donovan, in a 2007 interview in *The Desert Sun*, said of his decades-long involvement with TM: "I've been meditating, trying other forms and finding TM to be the most instant and important. Many other forms of meditation require longer periods and often retreat from life. With TM, you remain in life."

Mike Love of the Beach Boys learned Transcendental Meditation directly from Maharishi in Paris in the late '60s and has practiced it ever since. In a 2010 interview he stated, "When you're grounded in your self, the bigger Self, then your actions are supported accordingly." He became a teacher of TM on a course in Majorca, Spain, with Maharishi in 1972.

Speaking about creativity, he said, "Some people get self-medicated with alcohol or drugs. I would recommend to at least try TM regularly...With TM there is a way to feel relaxed, more clarity, and you're able to make better decisions. It's such a simple technique that anyone can do it."

In an interview with *GQ* magazine, Clint Eastwood said, "I think it's amazing how many people practice Transcendental Meditation every day, year after year. I think I know how they feel, and why they spend the time transcending every day— because it makes them feel more alive, more together, and better able to keep going and growing." He went on to say that it reminded him of something Maharishi wrote in his book *The Science of Being and Art of Living*:

"Expansion of happiness is the purpose of life, and evolution is the process through which it is fulfilled...If one is not happy, one has lost the very purpose of life. If one is not constantly developing his intelligence, power, creativity, peace, and happiness, then he has lost the very purpose of life. Life is not meant to be lived in dullness, idleness, and suffering; these do not belong to the essential nature of life."

In an interview with radio and TV celebrity Howard Stern, David Letterman said, "One of the things I have admired about you is that you meditate." He continued, "If I could learn to meditate, I know it would help me. I just don't want to go to someplace where people are sitting around without their shoes making 'hhmmmmm'—I don't want to do that."

Howard replied: "It's not like that. I [learned when I] was eighteen years old. I was in college. My mother was severely depressed—her sister had died, and she took it very, very hard. I was worried about her...I get a call one day from this happy, elated woman, and I wonder, 'Who is this?' and it's my mother. She tells me she was watching the Johnny Carson show, and she saw Maharishi Mahesh Yogi, and she went on and learned Transcendental Meditation. My mother sounded transformed. She said to me, 'Come on, I want to take you down to the TM Center.' I did it. And it's the easiest thing I ever did. I have been doing it since I was eighteen. I love to do it after the show. I find it very relaxing."

Howard Stern is an outspoken proponent of the Transcendental Meditation technique and strong supporter of the David Lynch Foundation's global initiative to teach one million at-risk students to meditate. In 2006, *Time* magazine featured Howard in its "Time 100" list—its annual list of the 100 most influential people in the world. He also ranked seventh that year in *Forbes*'s "World's Most Powerful Celebrities" list.

Some of the other public figures, both living and passed, who have acknowledged that they practice Transcendental Meditation include scientist, futurist, and visionary Buckminster Fuller, American jazz flutist and pioneer of New Age music Paul Horn, Mick Jagger, Shirley MacLaine, Burt Reynolds, Ravi Shankar, Kurt Vonnegut, Stevie Wonder, singer-songwriter and actress Patti LaBelle, and famed football player Joe Namath, who said,

"As a football player, I found that Transcendental Meditation helped me relax, and with a clear mind, I played better."

Successful hip-hop promoter and entrepreneur Russell Simmons, speaking to students in public schools in Washington, DC, said, "We need to get connected to our calm, relaxed, perfect self...It is such a blissful, calm place...when you open your eyes, if you operate from that calm place, then all that is supposed to be hard becomes easy." In addition to speaking publicly about Transcendental Meditation, Russell Simmons has helped establish a transformational rehabilitation program for the homeless in New York City. He tells the clients, "Transcendental Meditation promotes stillness, and when you are still is the only time you can think...TM is the practice of touching that stillness." And "Success is when you can be in touch with that happy thing inside you..." The testimonials from the formerly homeless people who spoke on video of how they were transformed by learning TM can literally move you to tears.

Other celebrities who have learned Transcendental Meditation include actress Jane Fonda; singer Ben Harper; comedian Russell Brand, a transformed heroin addict and now strong TM proponent, who served as host for David Lynch's benefit at the Metropolitan Museum of Art; Arnold Schwarzenegger, former governor of California, actor, body-building champion (Mr. Universe and Mr. Olympia seven times); Sir John Harvey-Jones, MBE [Member of the British Empire], industrialist, chairman of *The Economist* magazine from 1989 to 1994, and former World War II submarine commander at the age of twenty-four; British Foreign Secretary William Hague; and Deputy Prime Minister Nick Clegg.

Most recently, a celebrity who has been described as one of the most powerful women in the world—Oprah Winfrey—announced that she has learned Transcendental Meditation. In December 2011, Oprah was featured in an interview with Dr. Mehmet Oz on his nationally televised talk show, *The Dr. Oz*

Show. During the interview, she discussed her life after *The Oprah Winfrey Show* and her aspirations for the future, including the very positive impact the practice of the Transcendental Meditation technique is having in her own life and in the lives of her four hundred employees, all of whom have been taught to meditate using the TM technique.

Oprah told Dr. Oz: "One of the things I did in *Next Chapter* [Oprah's new series which began airing in January 2012], I went to visit a town called 'TM town' and it's in Fairfield, Iowa. Would you imagine that in Fairfield, Iowa, a town with a population of about 9,500, a third of the town meditates! There's a traffic jam in Fairfield, Iowa, at 5:30 pm with mothers and doctors, dentists and lawyers, and engineers and clerks and soccer moms all headed to the dome [there are two large dome-shaped meditation halls on the university campus] in Fairfield, Iowa—people who look just like you and me—and they're all there meditating.

"And in order to prepare for doing that show I brought Transcendental Meditation teachers into Harpo Studios to teach me and my team how to meditate. So we started meditating. Seven of us led to seventy, led to 270, led to now everyone in the company meditates. Nine o'clock in the morning and four-thirty in the afternoon, no matter what is going on, we stop and we meditate.

"And that way of being 'still' with ourselves—coming back to the center—and recognizing that something is more important than you, it's more important than the work you are doing, brings a kind of energy and an intensity of energy, an intention that we have never had before.

"And you can't imagine what has happened in the company. People who used to have migraines, don't. People are sleeping better. People have better relationships. People interact with other people better. It's been fantastic.

"So the one thing I want to continue to do is to center myself every day, and make that a practice for myself because I am one thousand percent better when I do that, one thousand percent better when I take myself back to something bigger than myself."

Norman Rosenthal, MD, Clinical Professor of Psychiatry at Georgetown University School of Medicine, is the author of a book entitled *Transcendence*, in which he tells of the healing and transformations he has seen in his patients who start TM. After researching the "hundreds of articles in first-rate journals" supporting TM and confirming how it releases stresses in the nervous system, reduces disease, and lengthens life, he himself started practicing it, although only sporadically at first. One of his patients, who practiced TM regularly twice a day, admonished him: "Doing it regularly is what is going to make a difference." Realizing from his research that it was true, Dr. Rosenthal began practicing his TM on a regular basis twice a day. He tells us that indeed it did make a profound difference in his life.

Several years after experiencing for himself the benefits of TM, he decided he must write a book about it. "What we know about Transcendental Meditation," Dr. Rosenthal says, "is that it reduces stress, not just because we see it, but because we can measure it...There is more alpha wave strength...and there's more coherence, which means that the brain is working more efficiently...What TM can do is to settle down the nervous system."

Sarina Grosswald, EdD, an expert in cognitive learning, says about her work with children who have learned Transcendental Meditation: "Children respond very well to Transcendental Meditation. It provides a mechanism for them to be able to manage themselves."

Ray Dalio, financial wizard and founder of Bridgewater Associates, the largest hedge fund in the world, and who according to *Forbes* is the seventy-sixth richest businessman in the world, with a net worth of $13 billion as of 2013, learned Transcendental Meditation as a young man. Mr. Dalio appeared on *Charlie Rose* and spoke candidly about his beliefs and how he runs his company. He feels so strongly about the benefits of TM that he offers to pay one half of the fee for his employees to learn, and if they stay with it for six months he pays the entire fee. Most of his 140 employees have learned.

When asked about people labeling his company a "cult," he said, "When I think of a cult, it means 'Believe this.' ... It's exactly the opposite of that. The number-one principle is: Don't believe anything—think for yourself."

"This is a very practical thing," he said. "I just want to make sure that point gets across, because people think it's kind of an exotic thing or you light candles or have incense and that kind of a thing. I'm talking about a practical thing that makes life go better." He went on to explain what Transcendental Meditation does for him:

"I was about twenty and the Beatles were meditating, and I heard about it and they had a TM center in New York, and I came to the center, and I learned about it.

"I became much more centered. School was very easy for me. School wasn't easy before. As a result, I also became calmer and so how I would deal with the world was more like a martial arts expert in a sense that I could flow with things and understand them better and react to them better. I was more in control.

"I notice a difference from the moment I meditate. I can be stressed, or tired, and I can go into a meditation and it all just flows off of me. I'll come out of it refreshed and centered and that's how I'll feel and it'll carry through the day. *I think it's the single most important reason for whatever success I've had.*"

Janet Hoffman, one of the directors of the Transcendental Meditation program in New York City, commented on Mr. Dalio's remarks, "We are in a city where we regularly teach many people with high-pressure jobs. Ray Dalio's comments on the benefits he receives from his TM practice reflect the comments we hear daily. The reduction in stress, anxiety, and fatigue coupled with the increased focus, creativity, and energy seem to give people the platform they need for success while allowing them to maintain fulfilling personal lives. Thank you, Ray, for sharing your thoughts with the public!"

With one phrase, David Lynch has identified the essence of what Transcendental Meditation does for millions: "Change begins within!"

FIFTEEN

SPIRITUAL REGENERATION
OF THE WORLD

....

*Now is the time to accelerate the spiritual development,
because spiritual development alone will ensure
abiding peace and lasting happiness...Spiritual development
is the process which brings to light and to our direct
experience, the hitherto unknown and unexperienced glories
of the subtler aspects of our being...Spiritual development is
the process of revelation of the ultimate truth of our life.*

MAHARISHI,
BEACON LIGHT OF THE HIMALAYAS

The fact that Transcendental Meditation comes from a tradition that is thousands of years old, tested by time and the experience of millions of people, is reassuring to me. This is not an esoteric technique cooked up by some well-meaning guru or public relations enthusiast late last week and served to us today as the freshest and newest way to "find ourselves." The fact that Maharishi Mahesh Yogi has written two major books, *The Science of Being and the Art of Living*, and his *Translation and Commentary on the Bhagavad-Gita, Chapters 1–6*, which outline his "rediscovery" of this technique from the Vedic tradition and apply it to our modern life, is significant to me. Hearing his history and experiencing his enlightened discourse, as he relates TM to each of us in our daily life and spiritual development, is inspiring to me. His plan for Spiritual Regeneration of the World and the success it has met with people of all cultures, from Russia to China, Thailand to New York City, is momentous in the life of the world.

• • •

Andrew Olendzki, a psychologist trained in Buddhism, points out an interesting distinction in his book *Unlimiting Mind*, a distinction between the Eastern and Western approaches to spiritual development: "In the West we tend to look outward and upward for our spiritual sustenance. The tradition of the East looks inward."

It is a tradition in India that those desiring to follow the path of the spiritual life shall find a master as a teacher and guide on their path to enlightenment. It is this tradition that Maharishi followed upon completing his university education in physics in 1942 and committing to serve Guru Dev. He spent many years at the feet of his master, an enlightened sage and recognized spiritual leader of India, before having the impulse to travel to the south of India on a pilgrimage. There he began lecturing and speaking about his growing conviction that "Something should be done so that people don't suffer, because there is no reason to suffer," and he began teaching his technique of Transcendental Meditation.

Maharishi's thoughts were recorded in a history of the early years of his Movement, *Thirty Years Around the World*:

"The Vedic Tradition, upheld in its purity by a long history of custodians, enshrines the supreme knowledge of the integration of life. From time to time, a revival of man's understanding of the eternal wisdom of this Holy Tradition arises to rescue him from suffering, restoring him to the speedy path of evolution, and awakening him to a meaningful life in Fulfillment."

Again from *Thirty Years Around the World*: "Everywhere Maharishi's message was the same—the suffering and misery so common to human existence are unnecessary. Life in its essential nature is bliss, and every person can experience unbounded bliss consciousness and integrate it into daily life through the effortless practice of Transcendental Meditation...

"Contrary to common understanding, no withdrawal from the responsibility of life is needed to gain enlightenment, to integrate the inner fullness with the outer fullness. Every person is born to enjoy 200 per cent of life: material and divine."

It is this message that he consistently brought to mankind as he taught hundreds and then thousands of average, ordinary people to meditate using his effortless system of Transcendental Meditation.

Maharishi's inspired followers later compiled his original lectures in a book, *Beacon Light of the Himalayas,* which records the kernel of his thoughts and the founding of his Spiritual Regeneration Movement based on the technique of Transcendental Meditation.

While the language of his initial lectures in India expressed the religious and cultural traditions of his country, it is Maharishi's unique contribution that he was able to transcend the religious vocabulary of his concepts and make them accessible to those of any religion, any belief system, any culture, in a manner that anyone can relate to. He made the following points in his initial lectures:

"Spiritual development is the process of unfolding the essential nature of the soul and bringing it out to light from the hidden chambers of ignorance—ignorance that stands as a covering and hides the subtle and glorified aspect of our inner personality... Spiritual development is the process of revelation of the ultimate truth of our life...to enjoy all aspects of life, material and divine... [It] is the process of bringing out the great fountain-head of peace and joy hidden with us."

He explains that this system of meditation is open to all. It is not the just for the hermit in his cave. Everyone can enjoy it; it is our natural birthright.

"In the most natural manner everybody has every right to enjoy permanent peace, Bliss Eternal, which is the nature of his own soul. Everybody has a birth-right to enjoy abiding peace and unbounded joy which is the essential nature of his own soul. And I hold Everybody already possesses the capacity of enjoying it, because it is already there in the innermost recess of everybody's heart. Nothing from outside can stop a man from experiencing the nature of his own soul. Nothing from outside can stop a man from enjoying lasting peace and permanent joy in life, for, it is the essential nature of his own soul."

This system is not an illusion. It is a formula that works for all. It brings us from suffering to permanent peace and joy. Anyone can do it.

"I believe in something practical. Mere talks of peace and fussing over it have no practical value in any field of life. If one peaceless and miserable man of the world could be made peaceful and happy, it would mean something of value, positive and concrete for the suffering humanity. If a formula could be brought out to light, a formula for transforming peacelessness and miseries of life into peace and joy of a permanent nature, that would be a boon to society and for the whole of mankind."

Maharishi instructed his audience one by one on how to meditate according to his simple, effortless system.

"By a perfect system of spiritual development, the great sages of yore have given to us the keys to lay open the treasures of great energy and power hidden within us. The Mundaka Upanishad declares that anybody who establishes himself on the highest attitude of spiritualism becomes capable of developing his will-power and mental force to such a great extent that he can attain any object or get into any strata of the universe by a mere 'SANKALPA' or a thought."

From his education in physics, Maharishi was able to see the connection between modern science and the spiritual knowledge he had from the Vedic tradition. He explained that the basis of all existence is formless energy connecting all of life both material and divine. It is this "Absolute" that we access when we transcend in meditation:

"The world of concrete forms and objects is made from the formless. This truth of Indian Philosophy has been supported by the findings of the modern science also. According to the electronic theory of modern science, electrons and protons are the ultimate reality of matter. [Remember this was the 1950s.] All these different forms of matter are nothing but involved energy. This solid concrete wall is nothing but abstract formless energy...All these multifarious material objects in phenomenon are nothing but formless abstract energy. No sensible man can refuse to accept this finding of the modern material science. Now if we are able to conceive that the whole material universe is nothing but formless energy, then it is easy to conceive, on similar lines, that all this concrete universe is nothing but Abstract Formless Brahman"—a term that Maharishi later comes to describe as the Absolute.

In one of the lectures that his followers transcribed in *Beacon Light of the Himalayas*, Maharishi described the problem confronting us. Something has gone wrong. We are missing reality and living only on the surface level of life:

"The Reality of life which is Anandam [Bliss] of unbounded nature is not at all being experienced...The most cherishable aspect of our being is out of our consciousness. What is the reason? Something seems to have gone wrong with our machinery of experience. Our machinery of experience is able to experience only one aspect, the gross aspect of the ultimate reality, and fails to experience the subtler aspect of its essential nature."

We are so busy using our mind—thinking constantly—that we fail to experience the inner (unmanifest) state of being that exists concurrent with the manifest state: two aspects of the Ultimate Reality.

Maharishi explains, "There are two states of the Ultimate Reality, Brahman—the unmanifested state and the manifested state." He continues:

"Our instrument for experience, viz. the mind, is constantly engaged in apprehending objects through the senses, which can only perceive the gross objectivity. Our physical eyes can see only the gross form. When the form is minute or subtle our eyes fail to perceive it and we need a microscope to see it. Similarly ears can hear only gross sounds. When the sound becomes subtle, our ears fail to catch it. Similar is the case with the other senses of perception. Because these senses can experience only gross objects, the mind, which is always experiencing things through the senses, is able to experience only the gross field of manifested objectivity. Due to the long-standing experience of gross objectivity, the mind itself has become gross and blunt. In its gross condition the mind naturally fails to enter into the realm of the subtlest "Anoraniyan" [the smaller than the smallest], and that is how it misses the Anandam [the Transcendent]."

What is to be done about it? What will the results be when

we experience the inner, unmanifest state of life while still living in the outer, manifest state of life?

"If the mind could be trained to apprehend the experience in the subtler fields in objectivity itself, it will definitely become sharp and in its increasing sharpness can definitely enter into the realm...and have the direct experience of it. The path [of spiritual development] lies therefore in training the mind to march through the field of subtler objectivity."

(In his book *Science of Being and Art of Living*, under the chapter on "How to Contact Being," the technique of Transcendental Meditation is described in terms of selecting a "proper thought" and experiencing its subtle states until its subtlest state is experienced and transcended.)

As Maharishi continues to explain in *Beacon Light of the Himalayas*, by following some aspect of the objective value of the senses to their subtler stages, we experience the subtlest stage in transcendence:

"At this stage when the mind is able to experience the subtlest in objectivity, it becomes sharp enough to enter into the realm of "Anoraniyan" [a field smaller than the smallest], which transcends the field of subtlest objectivity, and in this state it tastes the essential nature of that realm, which is Sat-Chit-Anandam [Sat—Being (Existence); Chit—Intelligence (Consciousness); Anandam—Bliss]."

As we quickly come to realize in our own practice of TM, this bliss is not an abstraction, but rather it is a direct and continually verifiable experience.

Speaking of why the spiritual life is not only for those who withdraw from life, Maharishi explains how the life of the householder living his life of activity and accumulation, coupled with the practice of meditation, is living as valid and effective a path to enlightenment as the recluse who renounces the things of the world:

"Obviously enough there are two ways of life, the way of

the Sanyasi [recluse] and the way of life of a householder. One is quite opposed to the other. A Sanyasi renounces everything of the world, whereas a householder needs and accumulates everything. Shastras [Vedic scriptures] declare both ways of life to be the paths of emancipation...The one realizes, through renunciation and detachment, while the other goes through all attachments and accumulation of all that is needed for physical life."

What Maharishi goes on to say may well be the most revolutionary aspect of his thinking and his system of Transcendental Meditation. TM is not an esoteric practice limited to those who lead a life of renunciation. It is not necessary to reject the material life to reach fulfillment, one need not withdraw into a cave, and in fact it can be totally nonproductive for those of us who are householders to attempt to live the life of a recluse:

"Thus we have seen that it is not at all necessary for the householder to go for a direct practice of [detachment or renunciation] for realization. That practice is unnatural for him, antagonistic to his nature and opposed to his way of life. If a householder begins to practice detachment in his life, he finds himself in a plane where he is not able to reconcile the mental attitude of detachment with his physical tendencies in life viz. one of all-attachment."

Maharishi sums up his approach to spiritual development for the individual living an active life in the world:

"According to my methods of Sadhana [spiritual practice—in this case TM], a householder can very well experience that great joy, unbounded."

Here he describes the process and the results of practicing his technique:

"Methods of Sadhana, which I am advocating these days, are simple and easy to practice. Everybody can easily practice in the most comfortable posture...in the morning and evening daily and soon experience the great advantages of it. Normally it does not take more than one or two weeks for a man to experience the great unbounded joy—called Samadhi or Atmanandam

[Transcendental Consciousness], and it does not take more than about seven days to experience calmness of mind or peace in day-to-day life. However peaceless or worried a man may be feeling, if he but starts the Sadhana [Transcendental Meditation], he is sure to feel some calmness and lightness in the mind from the very first or second day of Sadhana and he is sure to feel completely peaceful and happy within about seven days. This looks to be a miracle, but it is so. And the truth of this statement has been supported by the personal experiences of those who have seriously taken to the practice."

He again describes the results for those who practice his technique of Transcendental Meditation:

"Here is the positive experience of 'Heavenly Bliss' during [one's] life time."

And as for living in the present and enjoying the life we have, he points out that trying to ignore material life for the sake of spiritual development is a "fool's ideology."

"Select a path which will make you happier in your material life also. Do not live in a fool's paradise. Do not think that your sufferings and miseries of today will work as reservations in the galleries of heaven for tomorrow. Be peaceful and happy in the present and try to make this state permanent. This is the path of Deliverance in Life, Jeevan-Mukti [enlightenment], the most exalted state in human existence, the state of abiding Peace and Eternal Bliss."

It is this practice of Transcendental Meditation, which Maharishi brought from the Himalayas, introduced first to the East and then worldwide, that has opened up the possibility of "Spiritual Regeneration of the World"—to the religious, the atheist, the agnostic, the recluse, and to the householder. This simple path to abiding happiness and lasting peace is open to all, and it is what we are invited to experience by choosing to learn Transcendental Meditation.

SIXTEEN

GETTING RID OF WRINKLES

....

*The practice of Transcendental Meditation creates
a natural situation in the mind so that the mind entertains
right thoughts, useful thoughts, powerful thoughts,
thoughts that are cherished by nature and whose fulfillment
is worked out by all the laws of nature.*

MAHARISHI,
SCIENCE OF BEING AND ART OF LIVING

All of my adult life I have made lists of what I want to have, and do. For me these lists have been a road map of where I wanted to go, what I wanted to accomplish. I look in the mirror now at seventy years of age. I'm happy. I've had children. I've built buildings. I've been active in my community for many years. What lies ahead? Am I ready for it? A young banker said to me recently: "You've had a good run," as though at seventy, my life is over. Other than my repressed desire to take a swing at him, my silent response was, "Little does youth know." I feel strong and vital, and I will keep running up until the very last day. All my life it has been my plans and projects that have inspired me. I can look outward into the mirror and see the wrinkles now, but I can also look inward into the silence and expanded awareness I enjoy with my practice of Transcendental Meditation, and at some level I know I will be forever young and vital.

• • •

When you look inward, what do you see? You're growing older. When you look outward? The same. All around us things are changing. We ourselves are changing. We want to hold on to what we have. Is it worth it, all this change? We're rocking along. Buffeted. All around us is negativity. What is true? What is false? Which way is the way? When we are hungry, it is hard to think straight. When we are aching with pain, it is impossible to think straight. When we are enveloped in success and ecstasy, there is no need to think straight— we just ride the crest of the wave, buoyed by happiness and intuition.

Do we believe it, or do we not? Do we try it, or do we not? Our life requires choices. As we age, our wrinkles begin to appear. The perfection of youth's physical body begins to change. How do we react?

Consider that there are three levels of reality:

First is *physical reality*. This is the outside objective world. It is the wrinkles (or lack thereof) on our face and skin. It is the hard surface of a stone or the soft, giving surface of the water as we dip our hand into it. Physical reality encompasses the laws of physics, the boundaries and laws of nature of the objective world that we observe and move in every day.

There is also *social reality*. Social reality is the suffering of the poor, the enthusiasm of the rich, the scandals and successes of the political and economic systems. It is the greed and the beneficences of businesses and business leaders. It is the parties, the projects, the peace, the wars, the organizations and the structures of the society we live and move in every day.

Finally, there is *personal reality*. Personal reality is the reaction we have to our obviously existing wrinkles. It is the reactions and judgments we have to our encounters in the realms of physical and social reality. We like our wrinkles. They signify experience and maturity to us. Or we don't like them. They signify old age and our eventual death. Or perhaps we do not yet even have wrinkles. They belong to another time, a time we have not yet reached, or cannot yet even conceive of as part of life's experience.

Our personal reality is our own—the glass-half-full or the glass-half-empty approach to life. Which way do we regard it? What has our life experience shaped for us? Is life suffering or bliss for us? Maybe both? How can we be attached to life and all its stuff and not suffer? Everything, after all, changes. How do we achieve understanding? How do we achieve balance and peace of mind?

It is all so complicated, this living. None of us can avoid living in a physical reality. We cannot avoid living in a social reality. We can have varying degrees of influence and success in operating in both of these realms of our existence, but how we operate in them will be determined by our personal reality.

Are we ill? Are we overwhelmed? Are we unable to think straight due to the hunger, the pain, the misery we are feeling most of the time? Is that the basis of our personal reality? Do we regard our wrinkles as so undesirable that we cannot live with them and become obsessed with getting rid of them? Is that where our energy goes—focusing on our wrinkles, and we will not be happy until they are gone?

Our personal reality determines how we live in the world and society. Our personal reality determines how and whom we love, what work we feel drawn to undertake, and it determines our level of success in all our activity. What we believe, the thoughts we hold, the precepts we live by, determine the level of fulfillment we experience in life. Our personal reality and what we choose to focus our attention on determine who we are and what we get in life.

Talk is cheap. It is by our actions that we are known. What we want and what we focus on is what we will get in life. Where we focus our attention will determine what we get and where we go.

Think of it this way: Do you function better when you are happy or when you are sad?

Do you function more effectively when you have a plan and a project, or do you function better and get better results when you are waffling about, suffering in depression and unhappiness?

Do you even have any control of your personal reality and how you function?

Do your wrinkles get you down so much that you cannot do anything other than worry about them?

Do you perceive yourself as a victim of circumstances and poor choices, or can you keep it together enough to plod down the middle way and get along?

Our personal reality can be a matter of choice, or it can be determined by circumstance. And when we let it be determined by circumstance, that in itself is a choice we make, a choice by omission. When we're depressed, we know objectively we will feel better if we take a walk. When we are not solving the problem or

finding success in our activity, we know objectively that by studying harder, maybe taking a break, having a conversation with the
right person—somehow, some way, solutions will appear. The
answers will come. Be patient. Continue seeking. Success will
happen. We have control over our actions, our decisions. We
have control over what we choose to focus our attention on. It
follows that what we focus our attention on will shape the outcome of what we are trying to solve or achieve.

If you had a choice, would you choose happiness over suffering, bliss over imperfection and incompleteness? Neither is an
absolute reality. Just because there is suffering in the world does
not mean that we have to accept it as the norm for our personal
reality. Life is incomplete and imperfect, but in our personal reality we can choose to focus on completeness and happiness. To the
extent we can do this without binding our self to it, perfection can
become the goal and the norm. When we do that, the wrinkles in
our life will tend to disappear.

We may not feel we have a choice in the matter. But we do.
When we realize that stress is the culprit, that stress is the block to
happiness and joy in life, we can look to what is causing the stress
and our resulting suffering. We can go for analysis and examine
our past, our parents, our boss, our love, our job, our handicap,
our imperfections, whatever causes of the stress in our life, and
we can worry them to death trying to find a solution—*solving
the problem on the level of the problem*—or we can introduce
the *principle of the second element*, "turning on the light in the
room," and learn to meditate with Transcendental Meditation.

We can experience for ourselves the release of stress without
focusing directly on solving the problem. By leaving behind all the
things that cause us to suffer—by leaving them behind for a few
moments and experiencing the thoughts and the corresponding
stress release in meditation—we can escape the problems. In a
way, we "go around" all those things causing our suffering. We
take a detour right past them, and that detour turns out to be the

main highway! When we come back to them after meditation, rested and alert, attuned to our intuition, and in touch with spontaneous right action, we are better able to see our way to their solution and dissolution.

Are we kidding ourselves? Are we merely escaping physical, social, and personal reality, or are we transforming them through changing our perspective? By transcending in meditation, we are dealing with the wrinkles in another way—getting rid of them *as they affect our life.*

From experiencing the peace within us, however briefly, we come out refreshed. For a moment we see clearly, no longer "through a glass darkly." By releasing the stress in our life through TM, we are better able to deal with the problems of the world. The wrinkles are no longer of primary importance. They do not occupy our thoughts, our attention, or our outlook on who we are and how the world is. We will have gotten rid of them as they affect our life. And once we are no longer consumed by the fear, the suffering, the remorse of life's imperfections and harsh realities, the negativity eases up and ceases to have such a strong effect in the realm of our personal reality.

We then begin to function more successfully in the realm of social reality. We run into fewer obstacles in the realm of physical reality as well, for we are moving in balance now in our activity. We have given up the world of extremes, of suffering. Suffering is not a noble truth for us. And lo and behold, the problems we identified in our analysis begin to solve themselves.

The problems we experienced in our past or with our parents, our boss, our love, our job, our handicap, our imperfections, all begin to matter less and less, for we will have released our focus and attachment to them, and they are no longer such a source of stress in our life. If there are residual aspects surrounding them, we are able to effectively deal with them with a clear mind—a stress-free mind. Psychiatrist Ron Leifer, author of *The Happiness Project,* in his recent book *Engagements with the World,* posits,

"It is not the past; it is the future and lack of hope and vision that depresses us." With each meditation we clear our mind, release our attachment, and enter into "the future" with enthusiasm and a focus on the positive.

We do not meditate for the experience in meditation. We meditate for the improvement it brings to our activity in daily life. Meditation expands our personal reality to the extent that we can begin to positively affect our relationships in the spheres of social and physical reality. We have, in effect, "gotten rid of wrinkles."

Is this a joke? Common sense tells us, our eyes and our reason tell us, that wrinkles exist. They do exist. Suffering is a reality of life, but consider this: Someone is drowning. We can jump into the pond to save the drowning person, or we can toss in a life ring for them to grasp, and pull them ashore.

If we can stand clear, think straight, and act effectively in the moment, we have the opportunity of saving the drowning person without submerging ourselves in their dilemma, without ourselves risking drowning in the mire along with them. If we are overwhelmed with the danger and the drama, we can freeze and do nothing. Our personal reality will determine our course of action.

It is a matter of self-preservation. We can observe this situation with compassion. We can interact with all friendliness, but it is by our actions that we are known. We can maintain our own center and our own happiness while still operating effectively in the imperfect world of suffering. We can choose to join Arjuna in solving the double binds of our life by transcending the supposed dilemma, sometimes with an "out-of-the-blue" solution and the moral choice.

Do we jump in and save the drowning person? If we jump in to save them, we face the very real risk of drowning ourselves. What should we do? What is the right course of action? This is a double bind, fraught with risk.

It is not that we lack courage, but by keeping a clear mind, by having released our personal stress through meditation, we are able to act effectively, in this case by serendipitously finding a solution—a life ring—and tossing the life ring to the person drowning.

We have "done our duty," this time saving a friend, without ourself drowning. By being clear-headed and at the right place at the right time, and by recognizing and performing the right action, we have performed our dharma. We were not incapacitated by our fear, our worry, or another's suffering. We acted and acted rightly.

We have expanded both our own and others' happiness. It feels good. Things will go well for us.

SEVENTEEN

OUR FINEST MOMENTS

....

Life has two aspects, relative and absolute.
The relative aspect is perishable and the absolute
is imperishable. In order to give meaning to life,
it is first necessary to bring the perishable aspect into
living harmony with the imperishable. This is achieved through
action according to one's dharma, which maintains existence
in a way that furthers one's own evolution and that of others.

MAHARISHI,
BHAGAVAD-GITA: A NEW TRANSLATION AND COMMENTARY
(Chapter III, Verse 1)

A fellow real estate developer called me recently. He is older now and was considering selling one of his buildings, a major part of his holdings. He wanted to discuss it with me and get my advice on the matter. Since my son is now managing our real estate portfolio, and I have given him my (corner) office in one of the historic buildings we renovated, I now have a small desk in my wife's office at the TM Center several blocks away in another of our historic buildings. We arranged to meet there. When I arrived, the developer was sitting in the lobby and had picked up a brochure on *Scientific Research on Transcendental Meditation*. "You do this?" he asked me. "Yes," I said, "for nearly forty years, every day twice a day." "Is this that Raja guy, the guru out in Oregon who had all the Rolls-Royces?" he asked. "No," I laughed. "Maharishi is the real deal. Everything he had went back to grow his Movement worldwide. He died in 2008 with nothing of his own."

We ended up talking more about TM than real estate, and he decided to sell his building. I suggested to him what a perfect fit TM would be for him, as he made this transition in his life.

• • •

In 1975, based on the successes of the TM Movement and the growth of consciousness of those practicing TM, Maharishi began a five-continent trip to inaugurate what he called "the Dawn of the Age of Enlightenment." He announced that the purpose of his inaugural tour was to "go around the country and give a gentle whisper to the population." During this tour he visited Ottawa and had a private meeting with Canadian Prime Minister Pierre Trudeau. He spoke to him about the principles of TM and the possibility of structuring an ideal society. That same year, *The*

Pittsburgh Press reported that "Maharishi has been criticized by other Eastern yogis for simplifying their ancient art."

Indeed, Maharishi Mahesh Yogi has "simplified their ancient art." The Transcendental Meditation program is available to everyone, wherever they are, living whatever life they lead, whatever customs they follow, whatever traditions and religions they are accustomed to. Maharishi has lifted the veil of the esoteric from the practice of meditation and made it a part of everyday life for millions of people. It is no longer considered necessary to withdraw from society to achieve the state of happiness and bliss brought about by the practice of meditation.

Maharishi has also been criticized for charging a fee for learning TM. One TM practitioner put it this way: "Water is free. It is getting the water to you that costs money." Maharishi has said in response to concerns about finances in the TM organization that "Money is never on my mind. When I created the World Plan to establish centers in every country on earth, I didn't consider whether we had the necessary money to do it, I saw only the possibility."

Maharishi's goal was to spread his technique to the entire world, to relieve the suffering of mankind, to bring happiness to everyone. Maharishi also said, "We cannot take away the economic aspects of the Movement...even though my message concerns the non-economic fulfillment of life. If initiations were free, we could not cover the overhead for spreading the Movement throughout the world."

His message took hold. People learned Transcendental Meditation by the dozens, by the hundreds, by the thousands, and eventually by the millions. To reach them, the TM Movement grew organically, from Maharishi's first lectures in Trivandrum after leaving the Himalayas, to founding the World Plan and universities and schools throughout the world, and finally his "Global Country of World Peace."

Although there is now a worldwide Transcendental

Meditation movement, TM is still learned one-on-one. It is still a personal and individual experience. Each of us sits at the table and enjoys a meal, even though little thought is given to the incredibly organized and complex structure that brings that meal to our table. Just as we may sit in our pew at our church, at our desk at the university or business, or in front of the machine at our job, little thought is given to how the structure of the church, the school, the business, or the machine "appeared" before us.

The exchange that makes things appear before us is money. Whether it is in the form of an offering, a donation, a tuition payment, or a paycheck to us for our services, the exchange is money. We pay a fee, or we are paid a fee. The question really becomes then, "Is it—was it—worth it?"

In 1983, a group of Catholic clergy in England contributed to and published a book entitled *TM: An Aid to Christian Growth*, in which they publicly proclaimed the positive effects Transcendental Meditation has had on their religious faith. I have met rabbis, priests, and ministers who have learned the TM technique and experienced its benefits. The world is filled with religions and traditions, all fitting their society, all grown from their ancient traditions, and all with their devoted followers who find personal benefit and security from following their practices.

With or without our religious orientation, many of us still live in a sort of mystical haze of "whatever works"—whatever we have been able to find in our lives to achieve a sense of security, unity, and expanded awareness—"whatever turns us on." We access Him, Her, It, or even Nothing in a multitude of ways. The internal ecstasy, the trances, the fulfillment we gain from a religious or ritual experience can sustain us, rejuvenate us, convince us that we are on the right path to salvation, to inner peace, to knowing what is true and right for us. From the snake handling of the Deep South depicted in Sargant's *Battle for the Mind*, to the ancient practice of imbibing the right mushroom, to bending our knees at the altar for the bread and wine, we can experience for ourselves a sense of unity and all-knowingness, of peace and security, at least for a while. Amidst the stresses, the hungers, and the sufferings of our varied lives, these escapes, these rituals, these beliefs and convictions, allow us to turn inward and experience our finest moments. For some of us they are real. For some of us they give release. For some of us they point the way.

But if we step back and look at ourselves from the outside—what then? Do our practices make sense? Are they effective? What results do they give us in our actions in the world? Can we make sense out of the mystical haze? Can the practice or practices we have chosen be rationally justified by their positive influence in our lives? Are they provable? Were they—are they—"worth it"?

Probably they are, or we wouldn't follow them for very long. They feel good. They take us where we need to go in terms of self-worth, or adding productivity to our lives, or adding to the love and well-being we seek, or they can simply be justified by the feeling we are in God's presence.

The research on Transcendental Meditation is considered by many to be groundbreaking. When in our history has a spiritual technique and its effect on health, success, and well-being been so thoroughly researched, quantified, and verified? There are more than six hundred studies on TM, many published in peer-reviewed journals and conducted at some of the most respected universities in the world by both meditators and non-meditators. Transcendental Meditation takes us deep within, and the results can be—*have been*—scientifically measured (see research results in Appendix A).

While research can sway positive or negative in its support of a subject, ultimately we are faced with making our own choice as to what is real, what works for us. It is a bit like studying the history of philosophy—study one philosopher, and we can be swayed by his or her version of the truth; study another, and we can be swayed again. In 1637, with his publication of *Discourse on Method*, Descartes turned us inward: "I think, therefore I am." Once we have learned to meditate and experienced the inner Self at our core, we might change Descartes's observation to "I am, therefore I think." This is the strength of experiencing Being through Transcendental Meditation. We experience this sense of Being, and we experience that it is from Being that our thoughts and thinking emerge to produce the fulfilling and meaningful activity of our lives.

We can base our life on reason. That is a good place to start, even if through reason we have given up dogma, the adherence to beliefs imposed by a higher authority: If we are, so to speak, "on our own" in this search for happiness, we may nevertheless have sensed there is indeed a force in life beyond reason, a force that opens up intuition, serendipity, life in alignment with "natural law," producing an emotional and spiritual stability that does not necessarily result from following pure reason. We may sense there is more—a necessary emotional and spiritual link to something, perhaps undefined but certainly greater than ourselves. We have only to look up into the stars on a dark night to realize our own insignificance in the greater scheme of things. We have only to hold close someone we love to realize how full life can be, and how do we research, explain, and justify that?

Transcendental Meditation provides a balance for us between the inner and the outer life—rest and activity, the Absolute and the relative. TM brings peace to those who practice it. TM rests at the junction point between a life of reason and a life of spirituality. They are no longer mutually exclusive. The personal health, emotional, and social benefits are fully substantiated by scientific research. The anecdotes from practitioners about the personal benefits of TM are too numerous to dismiss.

Critics notwithstanding, Transcendental Meditation has been and is a pathway to peace, productivity, personal fulfillment, and happiness for millions of people. In the thousands of hours of lectures he has given, in more than twenty books he has written on the Transcendental Meditation technique and the structure and growth of higher states of consciousness, Maharishi Mahesh Yogi has made sense out of the mystical haze for the religious devotee, the skeptical agnostic, and the outright atheist.

It is through the practice of this simple mental technique, twenty minutes twice a day, that the individual can experience, as Maharishi has stated, that "the purpose of life is the expansion of happiness," and that life "is meant to be lived in bliss and fulfillment for the individual." We can experience for ourselves that "Life has two aspects, relative and absolute. The relative aspect is perishable and the absolute is imperishable. In order to give meaning to life, it is first necessary to bring the perishable aspect into living harmony with the imperishable..."

The practice of the Transcendental Meditation technique dissolves the "mystical haze" for us and can bring us to our finest moments, both inwardly during meditation, and outwardly in our activity.

EIGHTEEN

THE HIGHWAY SIGN
IS NOT THE TOWN

....

*The art of using one's full potential is in harmonizing
the Absolute and the relative.*

MAHARISHI,
SCIENCE OF BEING AND ART OF LIVING

It can take a lot of courage, patience, and attention to slow down and experience where we are when we are there, and do what we are doing when we are doing it. Typically, we are rushing along, we forget to make the connections, forget to feel, forget to touch, forget to love. We allow ourselves to be too busy to get deeply involved, and yet it is the deep involvement—with where we are, with who we are with, with the tasks before us—which brings depth, meaning, and happiness to our lives. This has been my experience. Perhaps yours? Should we be slowing down?

• • •

Have we really *been* to Pittsburgh, Chicago, or Philadelphia, or have we just passed through their airports? Driving along the highway, the signs for New York, Boston, and Los Angeles are just that until we actually exit the interstate and get lost in the details, the bustle, the fury—the life of the city we have chosen to visit. Racing by, just looking at the sign, we cannot truly say we have been to that town. We must reach in and taste it for ourselves before we can say we have been there.

We know, though, that if we exit the highway in search of flashy experiences, we will probably be disappointed. We may find momentary excitement for a night, but it will likely be gone when the sun comes up. Exploring a city is like anything else. Its richness will come from time spent there, getting lost in the back streets and shops, the architecture and the markets, meeting and interacting with the locals. We know that the most satisfaction to be had from a city will come from settling there and existing in its culture. Only then, and after some time, can we truly say we have been there, that it truly has become part of us.

In our search, we may find a guide to show us the city. With a guide, we will surely find our way more quickly. However we do it, the longer we stay in this city the more we will come to know it, and the more familiar it will become to us. What was new and exciting in the first days becomes routine, but over time we find new avenues to explore, new shops, new experiences. We combine the routine with the new on a daily basis. After a week, we can look back and say, "I know this territory—that street is familiar to me," and we keep walking, exploring the new, but the assurance of familiarity is comforting. We can always return to the peace of the spaces we know.

The better acquainted you become with the city, the easier things seem to go for you. You can get across town more efficiently now. You know where the best shops are. You recognize faces. You need something, and you know where to go to get it. You find that your boundaries and your efficiency in the city are expanding daily. Things go increasingly right for you the longer you stay and the more familiar you become with this place and its energies.

Living in this town is not without its stresses. The traffic, the jostling, the noise—everyone is rushing. Seldom do people take the time to smile or stop to talk. When they do, it is a welcome relief—a brief respite in the business of the day. You may find areas of the city that are run-down and even violent. You can choose to stay in them, or you can choose to return to the more pleasant areas with parks and baby strollers, clean streets, well-lit shops, and friendly people. You may have chosen to stay for a while in these rougher parts of town; perhaps you're helping out in some way, but it is always reassuring to know that you can return to the places you know, where people are not hostile and life is peaceful.

If you stay in the rough and violent part of town long enough, you may come to feel that life itself is violent. It's your choice which part of town you want to take as your own, which part of town reflects your lifestyle. People without the resources may feel trapped in the violent life, without choices, but not you: You have chosen to get off here, to explore. You have learned techniques for coping. You know the best parts of town, and this is your town now—good and bad. You can choose where you want to go in it.

You talk with friends you have made. What is this town really like? Well, it's got its good and bad parts. It's a great place to shop. There are thousands of cultural opportunities. The dining and entertainment are fantastic, but there are some rougher sections. Is that where you live? No, and you tell your friends that you have been there, you've helped out there, but on a regular basis you choose to focus your activities in the more pleasant part of town. It feels better; you're happier here. If you surround yourself with suffering and violence, you know you may be dragged down. After all, you say, why continually expose yourself to unpleasantness and suffering if you can avoid it?

You made a commitment to explore this city when you turned off the highway. You didn't just drive on. Maybe you came as a tourist, checking it out briefly, or maybe you decided to live here, but either way, forever now, this city will be more to you than just a highway sign. Your life is no longer whizzing by at seventy-two miles an hour on cruise control. If you stayed, you are involved. The comfort you find in the routine you have established in your city is balanced with the excitement and joy of discovery as you round the next corner and find a new shop, a new restaurant, a new experience. You like it here.

Maybe it was just the power of suggestion. When you first arrived, a kindly fellow assured you that this is the town to live in. Here, life is blissful. You saw the exciting parts, but you also saw the rougher sections, and after being here awhile, yes, you could accept that life here could be blissful. You know from your experience that to a great extent you create your own reality. Focus on the negative and your life will become more negative; focus on the positive, and that is what you will get.

Would it have been the same without the guidance you received when you first came to town? You could have inadvertently taken a wrong turn. You could have been robbed and mugged, forever taking wrong turns in an attempt to get away from the violence and unpleasantness. What would your opinion of this place be then?

You look back and realize that the guidance you received when you first arrived here made all the difference. You could well have been sucked into the negative life, but thanks to the guidance you have experienced the better side of life here.

You have been given a technique that somehow colors your outlook on this town. You meditate and then you act. It's that simple. Regularly, you do your Transcendental Meditation and experience the restful peace and bliss, and then you act. You take your chosen action. You were told life here is bliss, and you begin to experience it. You take the time now to listen to your inner voice, your intuition. Daily you do this. You are drawn to those things that give you greater and greater happiness. Why not choose what you want and go for it?

It is comfortable here. You find work or perhaps start a business. You know many people now, and you are successful. You are moving in comfortable surroundings. You know them well, and success and happiness pour in. You sit daily and go deep into yourself, a space of quiet time. It is from here the ideas flow. You go within, and you come out rested. You walk down the street and the right person comes along—just the person you needed to talk to. You go to an important meeting or rendezvous, and the right words pour out—just what needed to be said at the moment. There is room in your life for the love you sought. Life is good now.

You congratulate yourself. Look what you have done. You have mastered this city, and you walk in balance. You are involved here. You like it here. The journey has been fruitful. The quiet time you spend each day pays huge dividends.

You've made many a deal from the creative thoughts that come when you are quiet within yourself. You've formed many relationships from the confidence and inspiration you feel as you emerge from the solitude and strength you find in meditation.

From time to time you question whether your good fortune is real. But you know from your repeated experience that it is all real—intensely real. This is your city now, your place, your routine, and you operate within its boundaries, yet they don't feel like boundaries to you. It feels as though you are at the center of everything. Your world reaches out from your center to the stars and the galaxies. The biggest of the big and the smallest of the small converge in you.

Success pours onto you. Ideas and thoughts appear out the blue, and you channel them into action. You find that many of the thoughts which come to you are useful, valid ideas for expanding your work, your love, your friendships, indeed all aspects of your activity. You use them. You find that you are doing less and accomplishing more. With minimal effort, you appear to be creating your own reality. You are spontaneously making positive, right choices, and stresses seem to roll away—all from the practice of this meditation. You travel widely, become more educated, study more. And yet what is this technique you have learned—this Transcendental Meditation that has proven so useful in navigating life in your city?

You have learned that it comes from the most ancient tradition of human knowledge—the Vedic tradition of India, some five thousand years old. You hark back to Western philosophies and religions—the great thinkers such as Plato and Aristotle, the Church that formed and guided culture and thought for centuries. Perhaps you have explored Native American thought—Black Elk, holy man of the Oglala Sioux, who said, "But anywhere is the center of the world." Or perhaps you have read Tecumseh: "Trouble no one about their religion; respect others in their view, and demand that they respect yours."

Where does truth lie? Hundreds, thousands of seekers, each finding her or his own way, each adding to mankind's knowledge and mankind's choices. Which of these choices are for you? On a personal level, how can we know? René Descartes finally put all his books aside and reasoned: "Cogito, Ergo Sum." Whatever searching you have done, you find that from turning inward with Transcendental Meditation, a sense of clarity spreads into your outer world: "I think, therefore I am," or, from your experience now, "I am, therefore I think."

You experience that the individual, each of us, is at the center of our world. We let the world unfold within ourselves according to our desires and our abilities, through the performance of our dharma, our duty in life, the performance that enables each of us to be all that we can be, do all that we can do in life. "I am, therefore I think!" And you experience that it is true, that it is through transcending that you have the direct experience of Being—the "I am" of life. And you experience over time that the longer you continue to meditate, the more this awareness of Being carries forth with you during daily activity.

Your turn off the highway was auspicious. This is your city now. You own it. You refuse to live the delusional life any longer—driving by city after city, fast in your car, mindlessly happy just in the driving, seldom delving into the depth and detail of life. You have settled down now. You have chosen a path, and you have set out on your quest to understand and experience your life for all it is worth.

You were shown the way, and with meditation you now lead yourself deeper into intuition, deeper into the experience of the source of thought, to the bliss within you. It shines forth in your success in the outer world, in the immense satisfaction you now enjoy. Never again will your life be undirected, sorrowful, or delusional; you look back and realize that, now that you have learned to meditate. Life *without* this twice-daily experience of deep rest, deep peace, deep bliss—that is what now seems delusional.

It is a delicate balance, this inner life with this outer life. Left to your own devices without a teacher, without a guide, without a technique for accessing this inner quiet, you might have made up any solution, latched on to any set of ideas that came your way. You might have gotten lost on the other side of town, or gotten absorbed in your self-centered bubble, suspended in the air, vulnerable to every wind that blows, until it bursts.

Avoiding delusion—falseness in your life—is of paramount importance to you. You want to be able to trust that your course of action is based on a sound and truthful basis both experientially and intellectually. You want a life based on truth. You want to know intellectually and *viscerally* that what you are doing is right for you—that your chosen field, your chosen mate, your chosen philosophical and spiritual base are right for you.

You do not want to become like Sargant's anthropologists, converting to some strange religion because the fervor induced by the drums and the dance gave you a cathartic experience. Life is too precious to waste in some byway or in someone else's dharma. You are shaping your own way of life, both through following tradition and by studying each new territory as it opens up to you.

This meditation you have learned feels good. You have been taught to "dive within." Intellectually, you are told that the place to which you are diving is pure consciousness. It feels open, immense, real, and it feels true to you. Maharishi has called it the *source of thought,* but what is it? When you reach a place of peace and quietness inside, what is it? How can you know that it is not just self-delusion? Should you not be out "doing good" in the world, rather than sitting selfishly in this inner space of peace and quiet?

It feels good to sleep. You do not question your need for sleep. You do not feel selfish for sleeping. You may question where you go when you sleep, but you wake up refreshed, and where you go is of no great importance to you. In the same way, it feels good to meditate, to go inward into the depths of your being, into this inner space of peace and quiet.

During the practice of Transcendental Meditation, you may find you are breathing very lightly. You are resting deeply. You may have a sense of expanding into the entire creation. Maharishi explains that through transcending you have reached *pure consciousness*—the *Absolute,* that inner space from which all thought originates. You have this inner space in common with everyone and everything. You find it so refreshing that you have no question about your being there and basking in it. Life can wait. In fact, this *is* the life you have been waiting for. And similar to how you might feel after a good night's sleep, you emerge from meditation refreshed from the experience, confident and full of energy, rested and released from the stress that was overtaking you before you practiced the Transcendental Meditation technique.

More and more, as you practice the technique, the peace and wholeness you experience in meditation returns with you into the activity you perform all day long, every day. You experience clearer thinking, for your mind is not clouded by the stresses of confusion. Your thoughts are becoming more powerful, and your actions are growing more efficient and precise. Everything Maharishi has predicted for you, you are experiencing for yourself. Your intuition and creativity expand. You experience more and more the ideas and inspiration that come to you from an inner voice. The synchronicity with others—thinking of someone and then the phone rings—the long-sought solution to a problem that appears totally evident to you as you wake up in the morning, the experiences Maharishi calls *support of Nature,* become a growing part of everyday life.

You do not begrudge the time spent meditating, for not only is it blissful, but it is preparing you for life in the relative—life in activity. As you grow more successful, as things start going right for you, it is important to remember that you did not do this for yourself. In a way you did, by learning meditation, but it is not that "you did it." You realize, this is not an ego trip. You are following a natural process, open to everyone, a process that is predictable, reliable, and truthful. This is a technique that produces a happier, more productive life for everyone who practices it.

You will quickly experience the power of what you are doing. Following Maharishi's proven formula is safe and effective, and will produce results in your life which you cannot even imagine. Balance is the key: rest, but not too much, and activity—again, not too much. Keep your life in balance by practicing your TM technique as instructed and then just watch as life unfolds for you. Happiness will expand, and you will learn, as Maharishi has directed, to "take it as it comes."

Your city seems populated now with happiness. You radiate happiness around you, and it is radiated back to you. It may not seem logical, but it is based on cause and effect. You meditate, get deep rest, and you are able to perform more effective activity. Meditation allows each of us to experience a state of happiness and bliss as our stresses dissolve and we dive within to pure consciousness—the source of thought. Each of us brings this happiness to the surface and performs more rewarding, more enlightened activity than before. Perhaps your friends and neighbors begin to meditate. Each person becomes part of a web of interacting happiness that spreads throughout the city. Indeed, as thousands and millions of people begin to meditate, a phase transition to world happiness will take place, and each of us can truly experience that the purpose of life is *the Expansion of Happiness.*

Your turn off the highway has changed the course of your life. You are no longer racing by. Through your regular practice of Transcendental Meditation twenty minutes twice a day, you have harmonized the Absolute and the relative in your life. You have mastered life in this city now. It is yours, and indeed it *is* blissful.

NINETEEN

THE DYNAMIC TENSION

....

Because one can perform it, one's own dharma,
(though) lesser in merit is better than the dharma of another.
Better is death in one's own dharma:
the dharma of another brings danger.

MAHARISHI,
BHAGAVAD-GITA: A NEW TRANSLATION AND COMMENTARY
(Chapter III, Verse 35)

As human beings, we are designed for love. When we enfold another in our arms, we are in a sense kissing ourselves as the energy and bliss of the kiss flow back to us. If in your embrace you try harder, if you get aggressive and demanding, the "magic" of your love will disappear in awkwardness. This is very similar to "trying to meditate"—interfering with the simple, natural process of Transcendental Meditation by introducing some effort into the practice instead of taking it as it comes. In meditation, as in life, if you try to force things, the deep connections fail to happen. You must move slowly and deliberately. It is more effective to approach it in a relaxed way, for the kiss to come back to you with depth and meaning.

• • •

As human beings, we are designed for accomplishment. We try, try, try to accomplish, but it is in the *release* of trying, not the *frustration* of trying, that we finally make progress. Meditating without attachment to the outcome, going within and taking it as it comes, allows progress to happen. If you are in a hurry to accomplish something, if you lack composure, or if you are impatient, then achievement will withdraw. As in kissing, trying too hard closes you off from the satisfaction of accomplishment.

When you attain inner composure, moving easily in your physical, societal, and personal space, ideas come. Creativity flows, and emerges in its full glory; your actions become more focused, and success is most often the outcome.

When you effortlessly transcend with Transcendental Meditation, the intellect relaxes, intuition flourishes, and your life grows in the qualities of friendliness, compassion, strength, and good health. Hearing, touch, sight, taste, and smell become more acute. You emerge from meditation ready for action—ready to fly forward in successful activity. You go forth with happiness in your heart, rather than any feeling of guilt, sin, or suffering. Which way do you operate most efficiently—with the grit and grime of sin and suffering in your gears, or with the smooth lubricants of happiness, bliss, and love? What you focus your attention on is what you will get.

How have you achieved the successes you have had in life: making the deals you have made, conceiving and raising your children, influencing social structures? Did you achieve those successes with equanimity, or with broken lives and broken dreams scattered in your wake?

A dynamic tension exists in the creative process of living—listening to inner direction and exercising your will, listening to reason and following your intuition, resting deeply and then performing efficiently, the Absolute and the relative—accessing the depths of creativity and then expressing it dynamically in the actions which lead to your achievements.

The personal reality you create for yourself affects your ability to function and influence your social reality and the physical world around you. Hopefully you are producing a positive influence, building a better, more joyful world for others, and thereby for yourself, for it is yourself you embrace and kiss, yourself and those within your sphere of influence. It is the lives you touch, and the lives that touch your own, that give your life meaning.

It is for this that you practice Transcendental Meditation. Lethargy, lack of vision, fear, inaction, inability to focus and move forward, all tend to disappear. You become better able to realize your dreams and perform your duty in life. Your heart expands. Restlessness and hurry vanish. Your stresses are released. The kiss is consummated. You love yourself through loving others. You love others through loving yourself.

Here is a way to close the gap, to bring into harmony the tension resulting from what is and what ought to be. Transcendental

Meditation is a way to self-correct in the midst of negativity, whether it comes from inside or from the outside. It operates at a level beyond rational analysis and allows you to draw on the energy, intuition, and bliss that exist within you in your natural state. It helps free you from being overwhelmed by the stresses in your life, which so often get in the way and cramp your style and performance—the stresses that keep you from becoming all that you know you can be.

And what is man's natural state when we have the stresses in our life under control? We lie curled in contentment, adequately fed, adequately loved, with our children around us, like cubs in a cozy den. Each of us is a distinct member of the world family, each of us is relaxed and eager, ready to burst forth, to romp and play on the fields and playgrounds of our lives, to fully perform our dharma, our duty in life, and thereby through successful, unfettered action, to experience *the Expansion of Happiness.*

TWENTY

MAHARISHI'S JOURNEY: WATERING THE ROOT

....

*Problems are not solved on the level of the problems.
Analyzing a problem to find its solution is like trying to restore
freshness to a leaf by treating the leaf itself, whereas
the solution lies in watering the root.*

MAHARISHI,
BHAGAVAD-GITA: A NEW TRANSLATION AND COMMENTARY
(Chapter II, Verse 2)

We come in from hard manual labor; we come in from heavy exercise. We take a shower. How good it feels. We get up in the morning. We take a shower. How good it feels. We snarl through the traffic, the conversations, the problems hitting us square on all day long. We come home and enjoy an embrace with our spouse, a hug from our kids, a wag from the dog. How good it feels—a daily cleansing, an instantaneous renewal. We don't need proof of it. We just enjoy the good feeling from being renewed, however it happens for us. We are ready to go on. We are ready to face whatever comes next. Wouldn't it be great if everybody on our block could feel this good!

• • •

It is Maharishi Mahesh Yogi's major accomplishment that he brought the practice of this ancient Vedic system of meditation to the West, and then through scientific research suggested by many of those who first learned TM he confirmed the validity of its effect on the Western mind—a mind so intent on following only the rational and provable. Through his vision and unstoppable effort, Maharishi has revolutionized the practice and acceptance of meditation throughout the world. What was seen perhaps as only a questionable subjective experience is now recognized as an effective path to peace, happiness, and personal accomplishment, compatible with every religion, compatible even with no religion. Transcendental Meditation is quite simply a spiritual path that leads to a flourishing of health and happiness.

What began as a personal technique for growth of the individual has evolved into an effective solution for many of the ills of society—crime, poor health, and ethical chaos at the highest levels. Maharishi has created and researched groups practicing the Transcendental Meditation technique that have lowered crime in cities, reduced war deaths, and allowed for peaceful political transitions. He has proven that the power of groups of meditators connecting with the Absolute can sway the world.

Many seekers travel far to be in the presence of an Indian guru to experience his darshan—a heightened consciousness radiated from his powerful presence. With Transcendental Meditation, we do not need to be in the presence of a guru to experience the light and energy of heightened consciousness. We experience heightened consciousness for and by ourselves from our own transcending through the practice of Transcendental Meditation.

Maharishi has made each of us self-sufficient. He has given us a technique that will lead us to spiritual enlightenment. You will not need to travel to find an Indian guru. You will find the "guru" within yourself. This is the experience that TM will bring to you. And for this gift to mankind, many have called Maharishi Mahesh Yogi a world guru.

It is stated in Vedic literature that "fear is born of duality"— our separateness from that which is all around us: our possessions, those we love, the material world. They are all separate from us, and we are so afraid of losing them.

The level of unity you reach in transcending frees you from the fear of losing your possessions, frees you from your dependent love, frees you from this sense of duality. You realize that you are none of these things. By experiencing deep rest, peace, and the Absolute in your meditation, you can return to your active life in the relative and gain the possessions, gain the wholesome unbinding love, gain the world, because you have experienced for yourself the interconnectedness of everything within the field of Transcendence.

When you have experienced this state of consciousness, fear dissolves, and every aspect of life is more enjoyable. As one long-time meditator described his experience of the Transcendent:

"I feel like someone who while rather mindlessly wandering

around the streets of life, gets directed by a stranger to a palace. And once he travels there, walking, taking buses, trains, cabs, whatever, discovers a place of such majesty and beauty that it surpasses his wildest imaginings. And after he is given a tour into its rooms and halls, the utter beauty of which are mindboggling, gets handed the keys and told to his utter amazement, 'Oh, by the way, this is all yours...you can live here now...enjoy.'"

Maharishi's journey is a fascinating one, from bringing the experience of enlightenment to the individual to bringing the possibility of enlightenment to the entire world. A book on the history of Maharishi's Transcendental Meditation movement published in 1986 and entitled *Thirty Years Around the World: Dawn of the Age of Enlightenment* provides deep insight into Maharishi's vision for the world. The book describes how, in 1957, Maharishi had been traveling for two years throughout India, lecturing and teaching his meditation technique to gatherings of hundreds and even thousands of people. At the end of that year, in celebration of his master's eighty-ninth birthday, Maharishi's devotees organized a "Seminar of Spiritual Luminaries" in the city of Madras. They brought together ten thousand disciples of Maharishi's master, Guru Dev, as well as other holy men from all over India.

Maharishi recalled this gathering and the inspiration for the founding of the Spiritual Regeneration Movement in a talk he gave some fifteen years later on September 4, 1972:

"I reviewed these two years' experience in India—north, south, east, and west—and said that this Transcendental Meditation is such a simple thing, and it is found to be producing effects in all parts of India...where the cultures are (so) different...Why can't we spiritually regenerate the whole world through this technique? And with that thought I just said it.

"And the clapping went on for about two, three minutes... about ten to fifteen thousand people in the open-air meeting. These words, 'spiritually regenerate the whole world,' came completely automatically, as if from the review of what had been experienced in these two years in different parts of India...And that was the start of the Movement. Just that."

Maharishi had spent more than a dozen years in the service of Guru Dev, followed by several years in the silence of meditation deep in the Himalayas in Uttarkashi. He had followed his impulse to journey to the south of India, and he had accepted the invitation to speak. In his lectures he had objectified his inner conviction that there is no need for mankind to suffer, and that anyone could attain inner peace through his technique of meditation—this total wisdom of life handed down through the masters of the Vedic tradition, which Maharishi received from Guru Dev.

Maharishi Mahesh Yogi made an unusual transition for someone who had lived in silence as a follower of a spiritual master. He moved from the inner life of dynamic silence and, through his technique of Transcendental Meditation, brought that life of dynamic silence to the outer life of dynamic activity in the world. He brought his message first to India and then followed his ambitious aspiration to bring it to the world. He reviewed what had been accomplished in the two years since he had left the Himalayas and had been teaching his technique in other parts of India. His goal was to reach the whole world with his message, and based on his progress, he calculated that to reach the whole world would take him approximately two hundred years.

What more could be done? He had the thought, "Go to the most developed country." His logic, as he described it, was that if a country was the most developed, the individuals in that country must be in the habit of adopting new things. His technique of meditation would flourish there. He chose America and Germany.

With the assistance of his many supporters, and with his announced goal of spiritual regeneration for the whole world, Maharishi left India in the spring of 1958 and embarked on his first world tour. He stopped for several months in Asia to lecture, teach, and establish meditation centers in Rangoon, Bangkok, Penang, Kuala Lumpur, and Singapore on his way to the United States.

In December 1958, he left for the U.S. His first stop was Hawaii, where his planned stay of two days extended to one month. One meditator described Maharishi's impact:

"Though his first lecture was to a small group, the response was so unanimously enthusiastic that within a few days he was speaking not only to large groups, but also over the radio, as well as appearing on television, and being publicized by write-ups and pictures in the newspapers...

"Maharishi's message is simple and direct, the essence of all great faiths: the Kingdom of Heaven is within you. He gives a specific technique which is a straight, unwavering path to the innermost reality—the Self of each individual. His system of meditation is unique to the East as well as the West in that it is easy and quick—only fifteen minutes in the morning and evening. He does not set forth any rules for living...does not advocate any list of do's or don'ts. Do whatever you are doing, but also meditate."

On the last day of 1958, the *Honolulu Star-Bulletin* published an article about Maharishi, saying:

"He has no money; he asks for nothing. His worldly possessions can be carried in one hand. Maharishi Mahesh Yogi is on a world odyssey. He carries a message that he says will rid the world of unhappiness and discontent—'the root causes of all vices and corruptions.' His message is that of 'a flower...a message of time immemorial from the awed silence and icy coldness of the Himalayas.' Like a flower, 'people should enjoy not only the outer beauty of life but the honey inside. My method is simple, very simple...nothing to be done...no preparation. It is one of Transcendental Meditation a few minutes each day—let the mind go inwards. I wish to bring all humans in the world happiness. This meditation leads to blissful peace and happiness. It is for all men—the rich, the poor, the religious—it is also for the atheists. There is no harm in amassing wealth or having comforts, but the glamour of material life is further brightened by the glow of inner Self.'"

In the first week of 1959, with the name of only one contact, Maharishi traveled on to San Francisco. He was immediately introduced into the community there, and people flocked to him for meetings, lectures, and personal instruction in the Transcendental Meditation technique. A group of scientists and engineers who learned TM with Maharishi suggested that research be performed to verify the subjective experiences they were reporting with provable, reproducible experiments related to the physical and psychological benefits of practicing Transcendental Meditation.

Maharishi agreed, and thus began the research which today has evolved into the extensive studies now compiled in the seven volumes of *Scientific Research on Maharishi's Transcendental Meditation and the TM-Sidhi Program: Collected Papers*.

David Orme-Johnson, PhD, chairman of the Department of Psychology at the Maharishi University of Management and one of the principal researchers in the world on meditation and its effects, was co-editor of this series for several years. He described the research as follows:

"The scientific research on the Transcendental Meditation and TM-Sidhi program of Maharishi Mahesh Yogi is the largest and strongest body of research in the world on any program to develop human potential. The more than 500 scientific studies [since expanded to 600] conducted at 200 [now 250] independent universities and institutions in 33 [now 40] countries and published in over 100 leading scientific journals have documented that this technology benefits every sphere of life: physiological, psychological, sociological, and ecological. The findings in each area of study have been replicated many times, and meta-analyses, which are the most quantitatively rigorous means to review a body of research, have found a high degree of consistency of the results" (see Appendix A).

During his time in the United States, Maharishi had recognized that to continue bringing his Spiritual Regeneration Movement to the world, he would have to replicate himself many times over.

Thus began his first three-year plan to train 25,000 teachers of Transcendental Meditation. Maharishi traveled five times around the world in the following decades, teaching and establishing centers for Transcendental Meditation throughout the United States, Europe, and Asia. Thousands and eventually millions of people learned Transcendental Meditation—one by one. TM remains a private experience taught by a trained teacher to one person at a time. Maharishi's message has always been the same: It is not necessary to suffer. TM releases the stresses that cause suffering. The Transcendental Meditation program can produce a life of bliss and happiness for those who follow the instructions for the correct practice of this effortless technique.

For more than fifty years of teaching Transcendental Meditation, Maharishi and his trained teachers have enabled each individual who learns TM to experience for himself or herself that the purpose of life is indeed *the Expansion of Happiness*.

By practicing the Transcendental Meditation technique, you will experience for yourself what Maharishi means by the phrase "watering the root." Indeed, as Maharishi has said:

"Problems are not solved on the level of the problems. Analyzing a problem to find its solution is like trying to restore freshness to a leaf by treating the leaf itself, whereas the solution lies in watering the root."

TWENTY-ONE

THE COMMON SENSE OF
TRANSCENDENTAL MEDITATION

....

*Each individual has to choose his own path and uplift himself
by his own endeavor. Others can at best reveal to him
the wisdom of individual and cosmic life and inspire him
to establish coordination between himself and
the universal state of Being.*

MAHARISHI,
POWER OF SILENCE

In early 2013, my wife and I spent a month traveling in India. The high point of our trip was the several days we spent at the Kumbh Mela, a spiritual gathering which for millennia has taken place every twelve years in the city of Allahabad on the banks of the Ganges River. Mixing in this mass of humanity was an impressive experience—120 million people came over a period of fifty-five days to "dip" in the Ganges. For me, it was a pilgrimage into consciousness and respect for the Vedic tradition.

What was most amazing to me was the number of gurus represented there. It struck me as a sort of spiritual trade show, where one could go and see every brand, every teacher, every path available for spiritual enlightenment. There were hundreds of teachers. Each one had a poster or billboard advertising his or her method of meditation. Typically, their methods seemed to involve withdrawal from the chaos of our daily life. Each one had a tent—some large, some small. It was as though every preacher from every church within a thousand miles had come to set up shop and to convert us to his path. It was moving. It was chaotic in itself, with that many people within a thirty-eight square kilometer area, as if one-third of the population of the United States arrived in Manhattan to visit Central Park. It was overwhelming, with the noise and food and thousands of boats of various sizes rowing out to take people to dip in the *Sangam*, or confluence, of three rivers—the Ganges, the Yamuna, and the Saraswati. The three rivers converge in Allahabad, and it is to that convergence that people come at all hours of the day and night to bathe symbolically in Consciousness.

My wife and I were rowed to the confluence and dipped in. Why did we do it? Out of respect for this ancient tradition? Out

202 | THE EXPANSION OF HAPPINESS

of curiosity? Because the friends we were with all rode the boats out to the confluence and stood on the sandbar in the knee-deep water? Whatever the reason was, we dipped in the Ganges.

The fact that Transcendental Meditation is experiential and not based on belief is important to me. I started TM forty years ago, convinced by the scientific research and conversations with a few friends who shared their experiences of how it made them happier and more productive. When I called to tell my mother that I was considering learning TM, she told me that she had been doing it for five years, that she had introduced it into her prayer group at the Methodist church, and that it was "good stuff."

I am aware of the Vedic tradition from which it comes. I can put it in the context of the Indian culture, which is very religious, very spiritually oriented. But for me, and as taught by Maharishi, TM is simply a technique. It is a path to inner consciousness. In Olendzki's words, I do not look "outward and upward" for my salvation. I look inward, and not for my "salvation," but for peace, security, clear thought, and rest.

What I realized seeing the posters for the hundreds of gurus, and listening to the loudspeakers blaring in a language I could not understand, what I realized seeing the serene faces of the thousands, the millions, of pilgrims at the Kumbh Mela, is that Maharishi Mahesh Yogi has distilled the essence and the goal of meditation into his technique of Transcendental Meditation. Truly, we do not have to "believe in it" for it to work. We do not have to sacrifice all we have and give up the world for it to be effective in our lives. This simple technique takes us to the essence of what millions of seekers look for in the rituals, beliefs, and practices which accompany the thousands of religions, denominations, gurus, and preachers available to man in both the West and the East. Which denomination are you? Which guru do you follow? Are you Buddhist, or Muslim, or Taoist? Are you Baptist, Presbyterian, Catholic, or Jewish? Or are you of some other faith, or no faith at all? It simply doesn't matter. TM sweeps the room clean so that you can practice whatever beliefs you choose. With TM you can experience for yourself the truth at the basis of any path, because the truth that accompanies inner insight is universal. It is what one achieves in contacting *pure consciousness*, and TM will take you there.

The key to the common sense of Transcendental Meditation lies in what I experienced at the Kumbh Mela. Hundreds, if not thousands, of gurus advertised their wares at this spiritual gathering. Each one had bliss and happiness to offer those who followed *their path* to inner happiness and enlightenment. But you had to do it with them—follow their path, their rules, their methods: Support them, and they would support you. While Maharishi was a guru, and while it was his darshan—his personal presence as a man of heightened consciousness—that initially attracted his followers, it is his technique that endures. Maharishi did not base his offer of happiness and bliss on "following" him. He distilled the essence of all meditation paths, indeed all religions that offer salvation, freedom from one's small self, one's individual limitations, by finding one God, or many gods. He distilled it into his technique, a technique for connecting one's small self with one's larger, one's Universal, Self.

This is not a technique based on faith, not based on believing in Maharishi, nor following him, but based only on performing this simple technique of TM. The "mechanics" of TM take one inside to a place of security, peace, and happiness. It is a technique which enables one to release the stress of worry and inadequacy. It releases us of self-consciousness and doubt, and we emerge fully prepared to perform, to skillfully *choose* and perform, the actions we need to do to sustain our own life and the lives of those around us. It is a technique one can do for oneself, once taught by a trained teacher. It does not interfere with one's beliefs or one's lifestyle. It enhances the positive aspects of our lives. It enhances our religious practice. For with a clear mind we can choose and make the most evolutionary, life-supporting decisions for ourselves.

Maharishi's achievements in the fifty-one years he devoted to the Spiritual Regeneration Movement are little short of incredible. Maharishi followed his inclination to leave his quiet life as a recluse in the Himalayas, and he moved fully into society, teaching his Transcendental Meditation technique and bringing to people throughout the world the experience that it is not necessary to suffer in life and that the purpose of life is the expansion of happiness.

On February 5, 2008, at the age of ninety-one, Maharishi Mahesh Yogi passed away at the international headquarters of his Transcendental Meditation Movement in Vlodrop, Holland. His body was flown to India, where he was given a funeral with state honors—the only Indian saint ever to be so honored. In place of the twenty-one gun salute customary for a dignitary, out of respect the soldiers silently lowered their weapons.

David Lynch was one of the thousands who attended the funeral to pay tribute to this remarkable man and the knowledge that he has given the world. In an interview while there, David Lynch told a Reuters reporter, "In life, he revolutionized the lives of millions of people. In twenty, fifty, five hundred years there will be millions of people who will know and understand what the Maharishi has done."

Maharishi Mahesh Yogi was truly a world guru.

• • •

One starts TM from where one is, not through a conversion experience, not from a sudden burst of light, but rationally, based on the research and perhaps with the encouragement of others who have tried it and found it effective. Gradually, as we meditate with TM twenty minutes twice a day, our stresses are dissolved, we normalize our physiology, and we regain the clarity and peace of mind we had before the stresses of daily life took charge. We find that at our core we are pure, unstrained, blissful; at our core we experience pure consciousness and bliss. At our core we are happy, and we can access this happiness through this simple practice of Transcendental Meditation.

Whether we choose to become a monk or to lead the life of a householder, by learning TM we set out on a path, a path we follow for ourselves, a path of simple meditation which leads us forward, a path which enables us to experience our own source of inner happiness. We are no longer overwhelmed by what life throws our way.

Learning Transcendental Meditation–
It's simply Common Sense.

....

For information on how to find out more about TM and to locate a teacher in your area, go online to www.tm.org.

To learn more about Maharishi Mahesh Yogi and his worldwide achievements in bringing Transcendental Meditation to the world, go online to www.globalgoodnews.com.

SCIENTIFIC RESEARCH ON THE TRANSCENDENTAL MEDITATION PROGRAM

The following studies only scratch the surface of the more than six hundred scientific studies performed on Transcendental Meditation, but these are some of the most significant that substantiate both personal experience of health and well-being gained from the performance of TM and the effect on society of groups of advanced meditators bringing coherence to troubled areas of the world.

Physiological Indicators of Deep Rest
THROUGH THE *TRANSCENDENTAL MEDITATION* TECHNIQUE

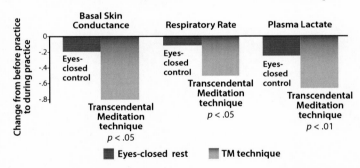

A meta-analysis (used for drawing objective conclusions from large bodies of research) found that the Transcendental Meditation technique produced a significant decrease in basal skin conductance compared to eyes-closed rest, indicating profound relaxation. Deep rest and relaxation were also indicated by greater decreases in respiration rates and plasma lactate levels compared to ordinary rest. These physiological changes occur spontaneously as the mind effortlessly settles to the state of restful alertness, Transcendental Consciousness.

References: 1. *American Psychologist* 42 (1987): 879–881.
2. *Science* 167 (1970): 1751–1754.
3. *American Journal of Physiology* 221 (1971): 795–799.

Increased Integration of Brain Functioning
THROUGH THE *TRANSCENDENTAL MEDITATION* TECHNIQUE

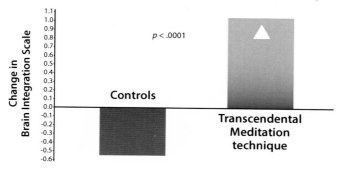

University students who learned the Transcendental Meditation technique, in contrast to students randomly assigned to a delayed-start group, showed significant improvement over a 10-week period on a Brain Integration Scale comprising several EEG measures during task performance. Components of the Brain Integration Scale on which improvement was measured included increased broadband frontal EEG coherence and more efficient preparatory brain responses to stimuli. Students learning the Transcendental Meditation technique also showed decreased sleepiness and faster habituation to stressful stimuli in comparison to controls.

Reference: *International Journal of Psychophysiology* 71 (2009): 170–176.

Optimization of Brain Functioning
THROUGH THE *TRANSCENDENTAL MEDITATION* TECHNIQUE

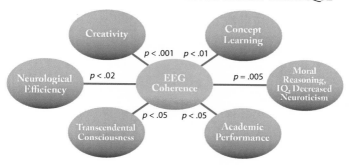

Higher levels of EEG coherence measured during the practice of the Transcendental Meditation technique are significantly correlated with increased fluency of verbal creativity; increased efficiency in learning new concepts; more principled moral reasoning, higher verbal IQ, and decreased neuroticism; higher academic achievement; clearer experiences of Transcendental Consciousness; and increased neurological efficiency, as measured by faster recovery of the paired H-reflex.

References: The chart above refers to data from the following four studies:
1. *International Journal of Neuroscience* 13 (1981): 211–217.
2. *International Journal of Neuroscience* 15 (1981): 151–157.
3. *Scientific Research on the* Transcendental Meditation *Program: Collected Papers, Volume 1* (1977): 208–212.
4. *Scientific Research on Maharishi's* Transcendental Meditation *and* TM-Sidhi *Programme: Collected Papers, Volume 4* (1989): 2245–2266.

Holistic Improvement in Intellectual Performance
THROUGH THE *TRANSCENDENTAL MEDITATION* TECHNIQUE

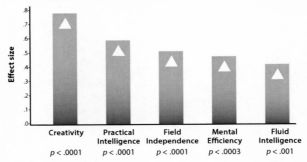

Creativity	Practical Intelligence	Field Independence	Mental Efficiency	Fluid Intelligence
$p < .0001$	$p < .0001$	$p < .0001$	$p < .0003$	$p < .001$

Three randomized controlled studies among secondary school and vocational school students found that, in contrast to controls, those who learned the Transcendental Meditation technique showed significant improvement in five measures of intellectual functioning; they also showed decreased anxiety.

References: *1. Intelligence* 29 (2001): 419–440.
2. *Personality and Individual Differences* 12 (1991): 1105–1116.
3. *Perceptual and Motor Skills* 62 (1986): 731–738.
4. *College Student Journal* 15 (1981): 140–146.
5. *The Journal of Creative Behavior* 19 (1985): 270–275.
6. *Journal of Clinical Psychology* 42 (1986): 161–164.
7. *Gedrag: Tijdschrift voor Psychologie* [Behavior: Journal of Psychology] 3 (1975): 167–182.

Improved Postgraduate Academic Performance
THROUGH THE *TRANSCENDENTAL MEDITATION* TECHNIQUE

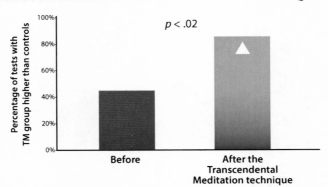

Master's degree engineering students who learned the Transcendental Meditation program showed improved performance on their standard examinations after six months, compared with randomly assigned control students from the same academic program.

Reference: *British Journal of Educational Psychology* 55 (1985): 164–166.

Increased Self-Actualization
THROUGH THE *TRANSCENDENTAL MEDITATION* TECHNIQUE

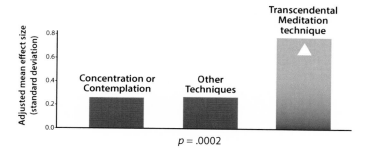

$p = .0002$

Statistical meta-analysis of all available studies (42 independent outcomes) indicated that the effect of the Transcendental Meditation program on increasing self-actualization is much greater than concentration, contemplation, or other techniques. Self-actualization refers to realizing more of one's inner potential, expressed in every area of life: integration and stability of personality, self-regard, emotional maturity, capacity for warm interpersonal relationships, and adaptive response to challenges.

References: 1. *Journal of Social Behavior and Personality* 6 (1991): 189–248.
2. *Journal of Counseling Psychology* 19 (1972): 184–187.
3. *Journal of Counseling Psychology* 20 (1973): 565–566.

Decreased Blood Pressure Among Hypertensives
THROUGH THE *TRANSCENDENTAL MEDITATION* TECHNIQUE

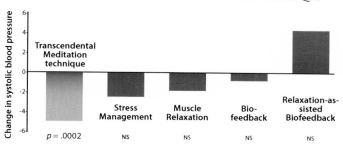

This meta-analysis was conducted on all published studies on stress reduction and blood pressure among hypertensive patients which met the criteria of well-designed randomized control trials with multiple studies for each treatment category. Only the Transcendental Meditation program was found to have a statistically significant impact of reducing high blood pressure among hypertensive subjects. A second meta-analysis conducted independently replicated the finding of significantly reduced blood pressure, both systolic and diastolic, through the Transcendental Meditation program.

References: 1. *Current Hypertension Reports* 9 (2007): 520–528.
2. *American Journal of Hypertension* 21 (2008): 310–316.

Reduction of Atherosclerosis

THROUGH THE *TRANSCENDENTAL MEDITATION* TECHNIQUE

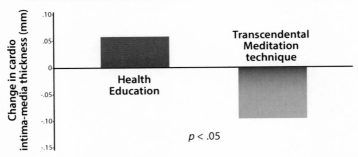

This study found that those who learned the TM program showed reduced thickening of the carotid artery. This finding was in contrast to continued thickening of this artery among a control group who took a health education program on diet and exercise for alleviating cardiovascular problems. Reduced atherosclerosis in the carotid artery has been found to correlate with less disease of the arteries in the heart and brain, which leads to lower rates of heart attacks and strokes.

Reference: *Stroke* 31 (2000): 568–573.

Decreased Insulin Resistance

THROUGH THE *TRANSCENDENTAL MEDITATION* TECHNIQUE

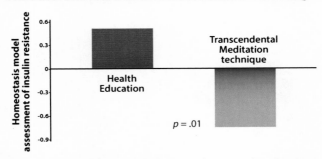

This randomized controlled trial found that four months of practice of the Transcendental Meditation program led to a significant reduction in insulin resistance among individuals with stable cardiac heart disease, in contrast to controls receiving health education. Insulin resistance is one of the components of the "metabolic syndrome," often associated with obesity, high blood pressure, and hyperlipidemia—a risk factor for cardiovascular morbidity and mortality; insulin resistance may also lead to type 2 diabetes.

References: 1. *Archives of Internal Medicine* 166 (2006): 1218–1224.,

Reduced Rates of Death, Heart Attack, and Stroke
THROUGH THE *TRANSCENDENTAL MEDITATION* TECHNIQUE

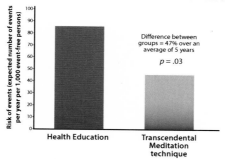

The results of a randomized controlled trial of subjects who had known heart disease and who participated in the TM program or a health education control group showed a 47% lower risk for death, heart attack, and stroke in the TM group over an average of five years compared to controls. All subjects continued their standard medical care during the study. Results suggest that the TM technique is a new, effective method to reduce the risk of cardiovascular disease.

Reference: *Circulation* 120 (2009): S461.

Decreased Hospitalization and Outpatient Visits
THROUGH THE *TRANSCENDENTAL MEDITATION* TECHNIQUE

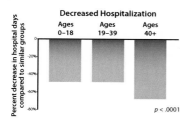
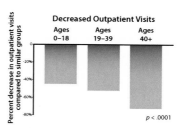

A five-year study of medical care utilization statistics on 2,000 people throughout the U.S. who regularly practiced the Transcendental Meditation program found that their overall rate of hospitalization was 56% lower than the norm. The group practicing the Transcendental Meditation technique had fewer hospital admissions in all disease categories compared to the norm (see chart on p. 15). The highest rates of reduction in both hospitalization and outpatient visits occurred in the 40+ age group, which normally has a higher rate of health care utilization than younger age groups, resulting in substantial cost savings.

References: 1. *Psychosomatic Medicine* 49 (1987): 493–507.
2. *American Journal of Managed Care* 3 (1997): 135–144.

Fewer Hospital Admissions for All Disease Categories

THROUGH THE *TRANSCENDENTAL MEDITATION* TECHNIQUE

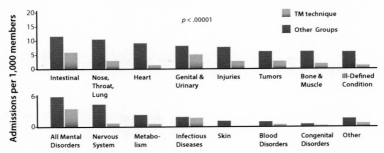

A five-year study of medical care utilization statistics of people practicing the Transcendental Meditation program (mean N = 1,468) found an overall 56% reduction in hospitalization rate compared to the norm. In terms of the leading causes of death in the U.S., the findings include –87% for heart and cerebrovascular disease, –55% for cancer, –73% for nose, throat, and lung diseases, –63% for injuries, –87% for diseases of the nervous system, including Alzheimer's, and –65.4% for metabolic diseases, including diabetes.

Reference: *Psychosomatic Medicine* 49(1) (1987): 493-507.

Reduced Psychological Stress

THROUGH THE *TRANSCENDENTAL MEDITATION* TECHNIQUE

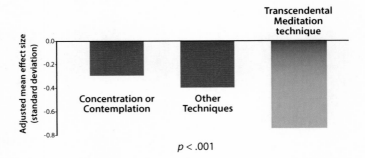

A statistical meta-analysis conducted at Stanford University of all available studies (146 independent outcomes) indicated that the effect of the Transcendental Meditation program on reducing trait anxiety was much greater than that of concentration or contemplation or other techniques. Analysis showed that these positive results could not be attributed to subject expectation, experimenter bias, or quality of research design.

References: 1. *Journal of Clinical Psychology* 45 (1989): 957–974.
2. *Journal of Clinical Psychology* 33 (1977): 1076–1078.

Reduced Drug and Alcohol Use

THROUGH THE *TRANSCENDENTAL MEDITATION* TECHNIQUE

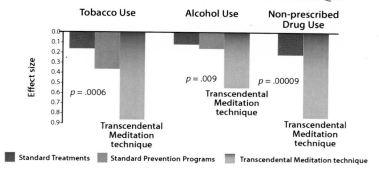

A comparison of the results of several statistical meta-analyses indicated that the Transcendental Meditation program produced significantly larger reductions in tobacco, alcohol, and non-prescribed drug use than standard substance abuse treatments and standard prevention programs. Whereas the effects of conventional programs typically fall off rapidly within three months, effects of the Transcendental Meditation program increase over time. The effects of the Transcendental Meditation program are spontaneous, based on fundamental and naturally occurring improvements in the individuals' psychophysiological functioning.

References: 1. *Alcoholism Treatment Quarterly* 11 (1994): 13–87.
2. *International Journal of the Addictions* 26 (1991): 293–325.

Improved Employee Health

THROUGH THE *TRANSCENDENTAL MEDITATION* TECHNIQUE

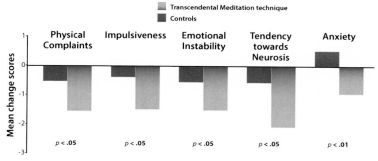

In a study conducted by researchers at the National Institute of Industrial Health of the Japanese Ministry of Labor and the St. Marianna Medical Institute, 447 industrial workers of Sumitomo Heavy Industries were taught the Transcendental Meditation technique and compared with 321 workers who did not learn the practice. The Transcendental Meditation technique group showed significantly decreased physical complaints, decreased impulsiveness, decreased emotional instability, decreased neurotic tendencies, decreased anxiety, and also decreased insomnia.

References: 1. *Japanese Journal of Industrial Health* 32 (1990): 656.
2. *Japanese Journal of Public Health* 37 (1990): 729.

Enhanced Job Performance and Job Satisfaction
THROUGH THE *TRANSCENDENTAL MEDITATION* TECHNIQUE

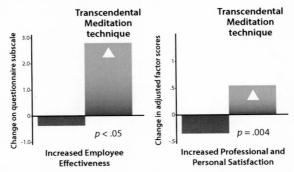

A study of executives and workers in the automotive industry found that after three months of regular practice of the Transcendental Meditation program, employees showed increased effectiveness on the job, as well as increased satisfaction with their professional and personal life, in comparison to controls from the same work sites.

References: 1. *Anxiety, Stress, and Coping* 6 (1993): 245–262.
2. *Academy of Management Journal* 17 (1974): 362–368.

Reduced Recidivism
THROUGH THE *TRANSCENDENTAL MEDITATION* TECHNIQUE

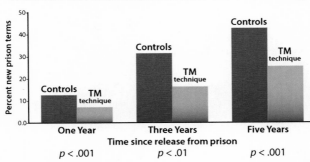

In this study, 259 male felon parolees of the California Department of Corrections who learned the Transcendental Meditation technique while in prison had fewer new prison terms and more favorable parole outcomes each year over a five-year period after release compared to carefully matched controls. The Transcendental Meditation program was shown to significantly reduce recidivism during a period of six months to six years after parole, whereas prison education, vocational training, and psychotherapy did not consistently reduce recidivism.

References: 1. *Journal of Criminal Justice* 15 (1987): 211–230.
2. *Journal of Offender Rehabilitation* 36 (2003): 161–180.
3. *Journal of Offender Rehabilitation* 36 (2003): 181–203.

Decreased Crime in National Capital Districts

THROUGH GROUP PRACTICE OF THE
TRANSCENDENTAL MEDITATION AND *TM-SIDHI* PROGRAMS

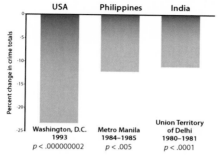

During periods in which large groups of participants in the Transcendental Meditation Sidhi Program exceeded the square root of one percent of the population, crime decreased in Washington, D.C. (daily violent crime, June–July 1993); in Metro Manila, Philippines (weekly crime index totals, mid-August 1984 to late January 1985); and in the Union Territory of Delhi, India (daily Indian Penal Code crimes, November 1980 to March 1981). The assembly in Washington, D.C., was much larger than the assemblies for the other two countries, with a correspondingly larger effect. Time series analysis verified that these decreases in crime could not have been due to trends or cycles of crime, to weather, or to changes in police policies and procedures.

References: 1. *Social Indicators Research* 47 (1999): 153–201.
2. *The Journal of Mind and Behavior* 8 (1987): 67–104.

Reduced International Conflict

THROUGH GROUP PRACTICE OF THE
TRANSCENDENTAL MEDITATION AND *TM-SIDHI* PROGRAMS

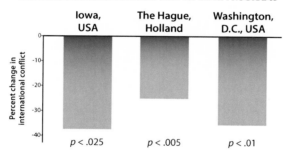

During the periods of three large assemblies of experts in the Transcendental Meditation Sidhi Program, which approached or exceeded in number the square root of one percent of the world's population, there was a significant decrease in international conflict worldwide, as measured by daily time series analyses of news events reported in the press. During the three assemblies there was also a significant reduction in fatalities and injuries due to international terrorism, as indicated by time series analysis of data provided by an independent research organization. Similar changes were not found in previous years during the calendar periods in which each assembly was held.

References: *Journal of Offender Rehabilitation* 36 (2003): 283–302.

MEDICAL EVIDENCE

Medical News Today
www.medicalnewstoday.com/releases/251668.php

EVIDENCE SUGGESTS THAT MEDITATION SHOULD BE INCLUDED IN GOVERNMENT-SPONSORED HEALTH PROGRAMS

More people still die from cardiovascular disease than any other illness. Dubbed the number one killer and the silent killer, modern medicine has been researching and incorporating complementary and alternative approaches to help treat and in some cases reverse and hopefully prevent this health problem at an earlier stage of the disease. One of those modalities is meditation.

A new research review paper on the effects of the stress-reducing Transcendental Meditation (TM) technique on the prevention and treatment of heart disease among youth and adults provides the hard evidence needed to include such evidence-based alternative approaches into private and government-sponsored wellness programs aimed at preventing and treating cardiovascular disease.

The paper, "Prevention and Treatment of Cardiovascular Disease in Adolescents and Adults through the Transcendental Meditation® Program: A Research Review Update" is published in *Current Hypertension Reviews*, 2012, Vol. 8, No. 3.

- In teens, the TM technique has been found to reduce blood pressure, improve heart structure and improve school behavior. According to the paper, the technique has been shown to be a safe alternative. The NIH-sponsored clinical trials conducted with TM mentioned in this review did not observe any adverse effects from TM practice.
- In adults the technique reduced stress hormones and other physiological measures of stress and produced more rapid

recovery from stress, decreased blood pressure and use of blood pressure medication, decreased heart pain in angina patients, cleared the arteries, reducing the risk of stroke, improved distance walked in patients with congestive heart failure, and decreased alcohol and tobacco use, anxiety, depression, and medical care usage and expenditures. The technique also decreased risk of death from heart disease, cancer, and all causes.

"These findings have important implications for inclusion of the Transcendental Meditation program in medical efforts to prevent and treat cardiovascular disease," says Dr. Vernon Barnes, lead author and research scientist at Georgia Health Sciences University, in Augusta, Georgia.

"This review is potentially more important than individual research papers because it shows that TM has an integrated, holistic effect on all levels of cardiovascular disease," says co-author, Dr. David Orme-Johnson.

Orme-Johnson says that no other meditation technique has been shown to produce this constellation of changes, especially when it comes to hard measures of cardiovascular disease.

Dr. Barnes said it was important to start preventing heart disease with adolescents before the disease sets. "Adding Transcendental Meditation at a young age could prevent future cardiovascular disease and save many lives, not to mention reduce the national medical bill by billions of dollars."

UNIQUENESS OF THE TRANSCENDENTAL MEDITATION TECHNIQUE

The uniqueness of the outcomes of the TM technique may have something to do with the mechanics of the practice of the technique itself says Dr. Barnes. "Meditation practices are different from each other and therefore produce different results. And this is a very important consideration when evaluating the application of meditation as an alternative and complementary medical approach."

A paper in *Consciousness and Cognition* discusses three categories to organize and better understand meditation. See Are all meditation techniques the same?

The two common categories are focused attention, concentrating on an object or an emotion, like compassion; and open monitoring, being mindful of one's breath or thoughts, either contemplating the meaning of them, or just observing them.

Transcendental Meditation uses a different approach and comes under the third category of automatic self-transcending, meditations that transcend their own activity.

The TM technique does not employ any active form of concentration or contemplation, but allows the mind to effortlessly experience the thought process at more refined levels until thinking comes to a quiet settled state without any mental activity. The mind is awake inside and the body is resting deeply, a level of rest much deeper than deep sleep. It is this state of restful alertness that allows the body to make the necessary repairs to rebalance its normal functioning. This cumulative process resets the physiology and shows up as reduced symptoms of cardiovascular disease and improved health.

BIBLIOGRAPHY

Dalton, Dennis, et al. *Great Minds of the Western Intellectual Tradition*. Teaching Company, 1992.

Durant, Will and Ariel. *The Story of Civilization*. Simon and Schuster, 1935–1975.

MacIntyre, Alasdair. *After Virtue*. University of Notre Dame Press, 1981.

Maharishi Mahesh Yogi. *Beacon Light of the Himalayas*. Sri A. N. Menon, 1955. Available online.

Maharishi Mahesh Yogi. *Maharishi Mahesh Yogi on the Bhagavad-Gita: A New Translation and Commentary*, Chapters 1–6. Penguin, 1967.

Maharishi Mahesh Yogi. *Science of Being and Art of Living*. Allied Publishers, 1963.

Maharishi Mahesh Yogi. *Thirty Years around the World*. MVU Press, 1986.

Perkins, John. *Confessions of an Economic Hit Man*. Berrett-Koehler, 2004.

Robinson, Daniel N. *American Ideals: Founding a "Republic of Virtue"*. Teaching Company, 2004. Audio cassette.

Sargant, William. *Battle for the Mind: A Physiology of Conversion and Brain-Washing*. Heinemann, 1957.

Schlegel, Karl Wilhelm Friedrich. *On the Language and Wisdom of India*. 1808. Quoted from Wikipedia. Thornton, Edward. *The History of the British Empire in India*. W. H. Allen, 1859.

Weiner, Tim. *Legacy of Ashes: The History of the CIA*. Doubleday, 2007.

ABOUT THE AUTHOR

Mack Travis, avid sailor, successful businessman, and civic leader, learned Transcendental Meditation in 1974 at the age of thirty-one. Since then, he has meditated every day, twice a day, using the TM technique. In 1979, he learned the TM-Sidhi program, an advanced program of Transcendental Meditation.

Both Mack and his wife, Carol, who is a teacher of the Transcendental Meditation technique, attribute their personal and business success to the calm and sense of balance they gain from the practice of TM.

Mack's first book, *Creating an Independent Income in Real Estate!*, tells his story of combining business and meditation as a recipe for personal success and happiness.